OWN IT!

How our generation
can INVEST our way
to a better future

Every owner of a physical copy of this edition of

OWN IT!

How our generation
can INVEST our way
to a better future

can download the eBook for free direct from us at
Harriman House, in a DRM-free format that can be read
on any eReader, tablet or smartphone.

Simply head to:

ebooks.harriman-house.com/ownit

to get your copy now.

OWN IT!

How our generation can INVEST our way to a better future

IONA BAIN

HARRIMAN HOUSE LTD
3 Viceroy Court
Bedford Road
Petersfield
Hampshire
GU32 3LJ
GREAT BRITAIN
Tel: +44 (0)1730 233870

Email: enquiries@harriman-house.com
Website: harriman.house

First published in 2021.

Paperback ISBN: 978-0-85719-830-3
eBook ISBN: 978-0-85719-831-0

British Library Cataloguing in Publication Data
A CIP catalogue record for this book can be obtained from the British Library.

Illustrations by robertsmithartist

Contents

About the author

IONA BAIN is a financial journalist, speaker and author who founded the pioneering Young Money Blog in 2011 and has since become the UK's go-to voice on young personal finance.

The Young Money Blog has won plaudits from across the financial industry for its innovative, witty, down-to-earth but clear-eyed approach to finance. The blog was named Money Blog of the Year by Santander Banking Group and Iona was shortly after named Freelancer of the Year in 2018 by IPSE, the leading association for the self-employed. Iona was also named one of the most influential women in finance by Onalytica in 2019 and shortlisted for the prestigious Georgina Henry Prize at the UK Press Awards in 2020.

Iona is one of the most high-profile financial journalists in broadcast media today, frequently speaking and presenting on TV and radio. She has presented special editions for Radio 4's *Moneybox* programme on topics like financial education and fraud, is a regular pundit on BBC News and recently became Radio 1's Money Hacker, where she advises young listeners on the station's flagship advice programme, *Life Hacks*. She also joined the economist Paul Johnson for a special four-part Radio 4 series, *The Austerity Audit*, in 2020; and other appearances have included *Question Time*, *Newsnight*, *ITV Tonight* and *Woman's Hour*.

Iona is renowned as a speaker at major conferences and is represented by JLA. She writes regularly for print and online media, recently becoming a writer for the *Financial Times* Personal Finance section, and has also fronted major campaigns for clients including Lloyds Banking Group, Post Office and Scottish Investment Trust. She wrote and published her first book, a guide to the millennial money basics called *Spare Change*, through Hardie Grant in 2016. Iona is the youngest-ever governor of the Pensions Policy Institute and a member of the industry's Next Generation Committee. She is one of the most respected financial writers and broadcasters of her generation, with a rare combination of accessibility and authority, and is often credited with bringing millennial money into the mainstream.

Outside of work she is a classically trained musician who plays the cello and piano. She is originally from Scotland, but now splits her time between London and Kent.

Introduction

CONGRATULATIONS!

YOU HAVE OFFICIALLY begun the process of owning your long-term finances. You have taken that first big step on the path towards understanding your money, what it does in the real economy, and how you can harness its long-term potential to boost your own prosperity and create a better world in the future.

Okay, I'm talking a big game. And maybe you have your doubts. After all, we are still dealing with the massive economic aftershocks of the Covid-19 pandemic. For young people, the future has never looked so scary or unknown.

Perhaps you looked at this book and thought: "This Iona woman is banging on about finance, investing, stock markets… but how does this relate to me? Can I really be arsed with all this?"

If you are thinking that, I don't blame you. About a decade ago, I would have thought the same. In my early 20s, I was a musician (I know, right?) and back then, I thought money was boring and grubby. I had my mind on higher things, darling.

But one night, everything changed. I was working as a pianist in a bar in Glasgow, which I was later told was run by some gangsters (good job I didn't play many wrong notes), and I would receive my payment in cash (that should have been a clue).

I put the money in a piggybank and kept it in my parents' house in Edinburgh, where I was living to save money. I thought I was being responsible and grown-up. Oh, the arrogance of youth!

On that fateful evening, my parents and I arrived home after they came to watch me in one of my Godfather gigs, only to discover the house had been burgled. Guess what was missing? Mr Piggybank – and the £500 I had put in him over six months. I was gutted.

It was only when a police officer came to take a statement from me, and I sheepishly informed him that I kept my money as a grown-ass 23-year-old woman in a piggybank only fit for an eight-year-old, that I decided things had to change. A few months later, I started the Young Money Blog.

Fast forward to today and I've written this book. What a turnaround! So, here are a few things I have learned since piggy-gate. Don't put all your worldly cash in a ceramic farmyard animal. Obvs. I realised that I should put some of my cash in a bank account to keep it safe.

But I soon learned that I was getting absolutely no reward for being Little Miss Sensible. In fact, I was LOSING money by saving it in the bank. WTF?

I was determined to find out more. As I continued to write my blog, I went deeper into the world of finance. I realised I had more choices than I thought. I started boning up on this thing called investing, which wasn't just for the Wolf of Wall Street, Dragons' Den millionaires and City boys in shiny shoes. It was open to all – if only I could get my head around it.

It dawned on me that our generation was already investing through our workplace pension. And we had some big calls to make about it, from how much money to put in to how we could use it to make the world a better place.

Meanwhile, technology and the internet were making investing more accessible than ever – but also confusing and perhaps more dangerous. As time went on, the penny dropped: somebody needed to break down today's sexy-sounding options and explain them all in an impartial and honest way. And that somebody had to be me!

So yes, this book is about investing – but don't let that put you off. I'm going to show you what investing really is and how it's relevant to someone like you. Because you have WAY more choices than you think.

Sure, we're still grappling with the biggest economic crisis of modern times. But arguably – and I know this sounds weird – there's never been a better time to start investing. You can get in at the ground floor of the recovery and help to rebuild the economy in a more sustainable, effective way.

You can allow someone else to design your financial future or you can own it. You can sleep on your stake in the future economy or you can own it. You can decide investing is not for you, that it's too dry, difficult and always for someone richer, cleverer and with better hair… or you can own it!

The choice really is that simple. Okay, the actions it requires may not be (that's why I have written this book!), but it starts with that all-important decision.

I can't and won't give personal advice because a) I'm not a financial adviser and b) everyone's situation is different. But I can explain:

- What's gone wrong with millennials' money – and how we can put it right.
- Why saving AND investing matter.
- Whether you should be saving or investing for your first home.
- What the hell a pension is, and how to make yours work for you and the world.

- How to use investing apps.
- The difference between various assets, fund structures and investing approaches.
- Important concepts like diversification and risk versus reward.
- How to manage your investing brain.

This book is split into two parts – the why and the how. Part 1 will passionately make the case for investing, even (or especially!) in uncertain times like these, and why you need to prep your finances for it. I'll discuss two big investments that may or may not already be on your radar – your first home and your workplace pension.

In part 2, I move onto the how. I'll chart the history of investing and analyse the different kinds of investment tech available today. I'll tell the truth about those must-buy investments you hear so much about (Facebook! Bitcoin! Forex!) before suggesting genuinely effective ways to navigate the markets – and all the emotions they trigger. I'll finish up by sharing the lessons I learned as an investor throughout the recent Covid-19 market turmoil.

Technical terms are highlighted in **bold** and I'll be defining these throughout the book. I'll also refer you to chapters where concepts are explained more fully.

What I propose in this book is that the younger generations can, and indeed MUST, use their amazing potential to give the world of money the kick up the bum it needs. We need to make sure our voices are heard, our values are acted on and our long-term prosperity is secured. We have to get more involved if we want better value and choices from the people marshalling our wealth.

Because it's not their money. It's ours. So, let's start owning it!

PART 1

Why should we Own It?

RIGHT NOW, YOU may be sceptical as to how much you can really achieve with your finances, especially after the enormous economic challenges posed by Covid-19. You may be unsure whether you're ready for investing, and more preoccupied with how to sort out your basic finances or buy your first home.

I'm guessing you have questions about pensions, what they are and whether you'll EVER be able to retire. You might have heard of this thing called FIRE – financial independence, retire early – but have no idea what it means. You might have a burning desire to do good but haven't fully considered what that means for your money.

Above all, you may be clueless about what investing is and why it matters. Be clueless no more!

In part 1, I'll look at why our generation needs to invest by taking you through:

- The economic factors that have held back our generation – and why they present a formidable case for investing.
- The importance of short-term saving and how to get it right.
- The areas of personal finance you need to sort out so you can be match-fit for investing.
- Whether buying a home is a valid investment.
- Whether you should save or invest for your first home.

- All the ins and outs of pensions, and how to magnify their benefits and make sure they fit your values.
- What FIRE is and what it can teach us.

By the end of part 1, you should be raring to go. But first, we need to look at the past decade or so to find out why our generation has struggled to own it – and whether we have any chance of reclaiming our place in the real economy.

CHAPTER 1

Why we've struggled to own it

LET'S START WITH a reality check. When it comes to money, our generation has been well and truly mugged off. In the past two decades, we have seen not one but two economic shocks that have disproportionately harmed young people. First, we had the 2008 financial crisis, which sparked a series of policy decisions and economic trends that put millennials at a major disadvantage compared to their elders.

Then, we had the cruel paradox of Covid-19. While older people were far more likely to be affected by the virus itself, it was young people (particularly generation Z) who bore the financial brunt of lockdowns and extreme restrictions on all our lives.

This book isn't primarily about economics, but it is the mother of all our personal finances, so let me give you a very broad overview so you can really get the rest of the book. I'll also be introducing some key concepts to warm you up and some ideas which may sound technical. But don't worry, all will become clear in due course.

Crash dummies

LIKE MANY OTHER millennials, i.e. born between the early 80s and the late 90s, I graduated during the financial crash, which roughly lasted between February 2007 and May 2009.

It was, at that point, the worst global recession since the 1930s Depression. A technical recession is where **GDP** – that is, **gross domestic product** (the main measure of economic output) – falls for at least six months. The UK's recession lasted 15 months.

The fallout affected millennials more than anyone else. We faced tougher competition for fewer jobs and had to accept lower pay. By 2018, people in their 30s were typically paid 7% below 2008 levels, while those in their 20s received 5% less. For the over-60s, average pay dropped just 1% from 2008–2018.[1]

Tuition fees were jacked up from £3000 to £9000 a year by 2012 and yet each class of graduates were earning less than the last.[2] By 2015 it was estimated that nearly 59% of graduates were working in jobs that did not even require a degree.[3] Pretty galling, huh?

Those who left school straight after their GCSEs during the crisis were even worse off. They were 20% less likely than previous school leavers to find work,[4] with their wages taking up to seven years to recover.

We have also faced a major housing crisis since 2008. Property prices soared, but housebuilding fell to its lowest level since the Second World War.[5] Banks became much more reluctant to provide first-time buyers with affordable mortgages. All this meant home ownership more than halved among 25–34-year-olds in some parts of the country.[6]

To cap it all, living costs also swelled, from the price of our daily commute to our household bills.[7]

So, as you can see, young people weren't in a fantastic place even before the Covid-19 crisis came along.

Something else that's proved to be a major financial buzzkill? The decline of savings.

Can saving be saved?

CUSTOMERS WHO PUT their spare cash in a savings account receive a reward known as an **annual equivalent rate (AER)**. This is a form of **interest**. If you save, you earn interest. If you borrow, you pay it.

Why do banks and building societies pay us to save? Because they use our cash to help provide loans, credit cards and mortgages to borrowers, who pay an **annual percentage rate (APR)** on their debt to cover all the costs and risks involved.

So, for example, putting £1000 in a savings account with an interest rate of 1.5% would earn you £15 in the first year. But if you borrowed £1000 on a credit card at a fairly typical APR of 20%, you would pay £200 (if you weren't on an interest-free offer, that is).

In times gone by, banks and building societies relied on cash deposited in their coffers (hence the formal name: **deposit savings**). All that changed post-2008.

The Bank of England (BOE), the central bank responsible for keeping the UK economy on track, karate-chopped the UK's national interest rate (usually called the **base rate**) to just 0.5%.

Bank of England base rate

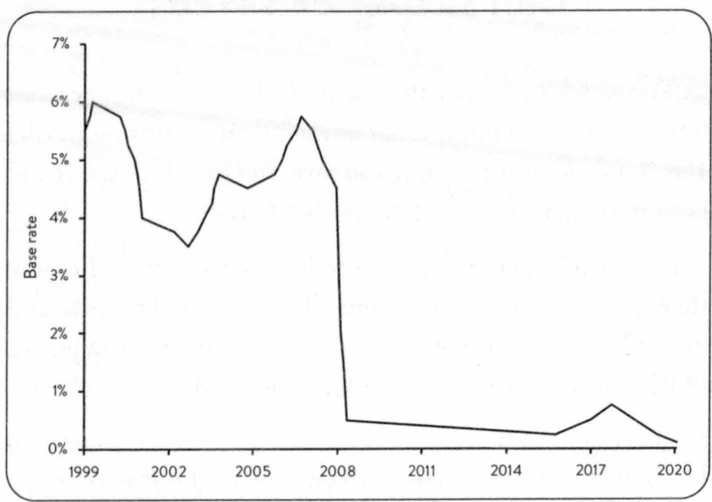

This eased the pressure on borrowers who didn't have to pay as much interest on their debts. But since the base rate is the anchor for ALL interest rates in the UK, it also prompted banks and building societies to cut the interest they pay on savings to virtually nothing.

What's more, the BOE offered cheap loans to banks and building societies, which in turn were passed on to borrowers and businesses from 2012–2018. This scheme, known as Funding for Lending, killed any incentive to reel in savers' money.

All this was bad enough, but Covid-19 made matters far worse. Prior to the pandemic, the base rate had crept up to 0.75%, but in March 2020 it was slashed to 0.25%, then to a new low of 0.1%, in a desperate bid to keep money flowing around the economy while the UK went into lockdown.

All this means that young people who try to do the right thing and squirrel cash away for the future are getting nada in return.

In fact, they're being slapped around the face with a wet kipper – and that kipper's name is **inflation**.

Let me explain…

Inflation nation

INFLATION IS THE rate at which the cost of stuff rises. It's measured by an **index** (or rather, various **indices**, plural) which is a number that gives the value of something now relative to its value at another time.

If the main inflation index – which is the **Consumer Price Index** in the UK – is at 4%, this means that you need £104 to buy the same stuff this year that you could have bought last year with £100. Inflation reduces the purchasing power of your money.

So, if your savings AER (and indeed your wage growth) is any lower than the rate of inflation, you are LOSING money in real terms. That's because the value of your money hasn't grown enough, even with interest on top, to keep pace with the rising cost of stuff.

Inflation isn't all bad. If we had the opposite – **deflation** – prices would fall, and consumers would put off big purchases in the hope of getting even bigger bargains in the future, and that would stall the economy. And inflation is great for borrowers (both individuals and governments) because if inflation reduces the value of your money, it also reduces the value of your debt. But when interest rates have slumped, inflation is the savings Death Star. (Cue the Imperial March…)

With inflation mostly higher than typical interest rates for the past decade, we've had a truly messed-up situation where people stand to lose money if they save it.

And remember, inflation doesn't have to be that high for savers to lose out: the base rate just has to stay rock bottom. This is very likely when it makes debt cheaper and might stimulate spending post-Covid, which in turn will probably push up inflation, further squeezing savers.

Economics: don't cha love it?

And there's one more thing to consider: **quantitative easing (QE)**. Try saying *that* out loud.

Pumped-up banks

POST-FINANCIAL CRASH, THE central banks used a new trick to try and revive the economy. They created new digital cash to buy a kind of **asset**. Assets are the bread and butter of this book – basically, they are valuable things we can own.

Lamonts Financial Glossary (oooh!) defines an asset as:

> Anything owned that is of benefit. Assets can be tangible (such as property, machinery, cash or investments) or intangible (such as goodwill, trade markets or brand names).

Like many central banks, the Bank of England has used QE (worth £895bn, as of November 2020) to buy a kind of asset known as a **bond**, specifically a **government bond**. We'll talk about these in more detail in part 2. For now, all you need to know is that central banks have done this to try and hold down interest rates across the financial system so that banks, businesses and individuals can use cheap loans to borrow their way back to financial health.

Now, the Bank of England argues that QE has been a boon for young people, raising the average household income by £9000 in a decade, as we benefit from businesses borrowing to expand and paying higher wages as a result.

Hmm. That's an *interesting* take. But let's consider how QE also raised the value of assets right across the economy.

How QE slayed millennials

AS INTEREST RATES dropped on mortgages (i.e. home loans), it boosted demand for property among those who could afford it – at a time when supply was already low. Property prices rose by 43% in the 2010s, far more than they would have done without QE and far higher than wage growth in the same period.

A more complex but equally important consequence of QE is how it raises the value of another key asset that is a BIG focus of this book. **Stocks and shares**, commonly abbreviated to **shares** and also known as **equities** (stocks, shares and equities are all the same thing), are individual slices of a company that you can own – like pieces of a cake – so long as that company is listed on a **stock exchange** or **stock market**.

Companies sell these slices to help raise money for their business. If you buy a share, you own a small part of the company and become a **shareholder** (or **equity holder**). The value of your shares will go up and down depending on what's happening to the company, the industry/country it's operating in and how well the overall economy is doing.

QE is the gift that keeps on giving for shareholders for many reasons. Stock markets go "yay" when central banks inject money into the economy, while companies can invest and become more valuable if they can borrow cheaply.

Quantitative easing

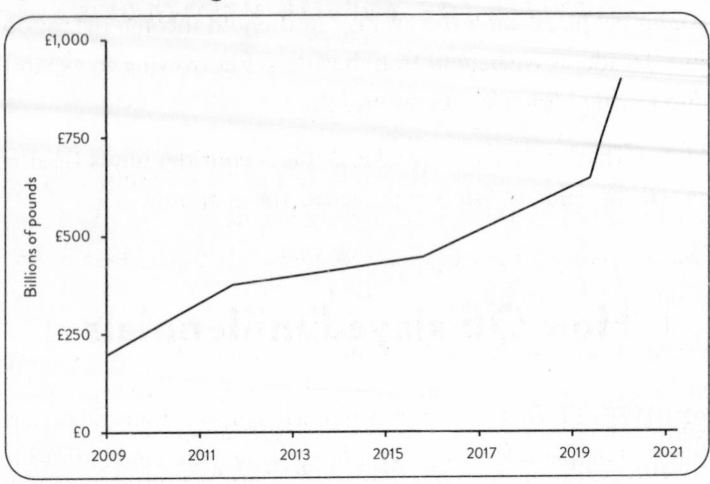

Plus, if people can't earn high interest on bonds or deposit savings, they look for better options elsewhere – like shares. Higher demand for shares raises their value, and more valuable shares raises demand for them.

It's easy to see how all this more than DOUBLED the value of shares listed on the **FTSE 100 index**, i.e. Britain's main stock exchange, over the past decade. Even after the stock market bloodbath of early 2020, market watchers were surprised at just how quickly share prices rebounded on the back of more QE, appearing to defy wider economic pessimism. Most economists now believe QE will become a mainstay of modern economic policy.

Who has benefited from all this? Shareholders and homeowners, who tend to be older people. Millennials have largely missed out on this whole asset-boosting orgy. Sniff.

Snowflakes versus gammons

THAT'S WHY WE'RE hearing so much about intergenerational inequality. And this itself is inflaming *intragenerational* inequality. That means there is a two-track economy among younger people. Those who can access the *Bank of Mum and Dad* are doing far better than those who can't. And that divide is only likely to widen post-Covid.

Young people from more affluent families are also more likely to benefit from The Knowledge. They beat the system. They know the ruses to get on the housing ladder sooner. They take advantage of the loopholes that allow them to pay less tax. They know how to get their costs falling and their long-term wealth rising. Around 9% of them even have second properties![8]

It's not just about having a bit more money (though that's always nice). It's about the inside track too. It's a sad irony that the young people who need the most financial guidance and support are the ones least likely to receive it. We used to talk about the haves and the have-nots: now, it's about the have-helps and have-no-helps.

Now you can see why QE is accused of promoting huge inequality, both between AND within generations, by inflating the prices of assets that richer, older investors already own.[9] But we also need to cut the baby boomers some slack.

OK, boomer: let's call a draw

YES, PARENTAL HANDOUTS exacerbate the financial differences among millennials. But what else are families supposed to do? Should they hold back in the vain hope that governments will step up? If our parents hadn't got involved and become one of the largest mortgage lenders in the UK,[10] where would many of us be now?

Plus, boomers have suffered their own woes, from mis-selling scandals to an array of unexpected charges and taxes on their pensions. And they endured the Wild West of banking and financial advice in 1980s–1990s. Bad boys in finance are nothing new!

Besides, we weren't the only ones screwed over by low interest rates and QE. Many baby boomers scrimped their butts off to pay down mortgages when rates regularly hit the double figures in the 1970s and 1980s. Was it too much for them to hope that they could draw on the interest from their savings in retirement? Seemingly yes.

And having all the natural advantages in the world is still no guarantee that you and your family will always end up on top, such is the minefield that is modern finance. Governments, central banks and financial firms shift the goalposts on savings, investments, taxes and pensions so often, even dodgy old FIFA would object.

People of all ages need to be as sharp as a pin to avoid being bamboozled, befuddled and burnt by financial firms, such is the level of jargon and mis-practice still being allowed by regulators and politicians today.

Don't get mad, get informed

NOW, YOU'LL BE relieved to hear the worst is over. Kudos for sticking with me.

At this stage I wouldn't blame you for, at least, feeling a bit down and, at most, having the urge to scream into a pillow.

This might sound a bit masochistic on my part but – good! A little bit of righteous indignation should fire you up and make you want to learn how to get the better of all this.

And look, I had to find a way to shock you. There are, like, a bazillion claims on your attention. Most of us are in a near-constant state of 'overwhelm' today.

It's easy to get depressed about your prospects when you glimpse headlines and see nothing but bad news. It's tempting to push this economic and finance stuff to the back of your mind. But it's far wiser to face things as they really are so you can take decisive action.

And really – what's the point in feeling bitter and hopeless? My motto on the Young Money Blog is: "Don't get mad, get informed."

Plus, there's good news. We have far more power than we think. Sure, there are problems. But there are also solutions waiting to be discovered if you just turn the page…

ST. MOGGIES CAT HOME
GENEROUSLY FUNDED BY
YOUR INHERITANCE

CHAPTER 2

What we can do about it!

OKAY, WE'VE ESTABLISHED that young people have faced a lot of pain in the last decade, and it continues today. But it's not all doom and gloom. Modern life offers our generation an incredible degree of self-education, amenities and choice.

Our parents' world was more limited than ours, especially for women. To think that when my mum was my age (30), a pub could legally refuse to serve her if she was the one buying a round (this only changed in 1982)!

We can learn, earn, upskill, work flexibly and optimise our finances like never before. In other words, we have a genuine chance to really own our future.

There are five big reasons why we matter.

1. **Millennials belong to the biggest generational cohort since the boomers.** We make up more than a third of the modern workforce.[11] We spend more than any generation on food, fuel, phone bills and other basics.[12] That makes us a collective force to be reckoned with.

2. **We are in the driving seat when interacting with brands – financial or otherwise.** Where our parents had to be loyal to a limited choice of companies, we can be fickle. Technology is progressing at its most rapid rate in history, improving access to and quality of services all the time.

3. **A universe of information is now at our fingertips.** Alongside the mainstream sources are alternatives, including citizen journalism, consumer reviews and in-depth commentary of the likes never previously available. They are full of tripwires, sure. But young people who know what to consider (and what to discount) can chart a path through it all – and come out more empowered as a result.
4. **We can be value conscious.** This doesn't mean chasing the lowest costs above all else. What I'm talking about is weighing up costs accurately so we shouldn't pay more than is necessary. I won't pretend we are in a utopia where all costs are easy to compare. But things are slowly getting better and young people can take advantage.
5. **Some of us have actually got some cold, hard cash coming our way.** Millennials are in line for a future £5.5 trillion windfall from baby boomers[13] and five million people aged between 25 and 45 reckon their inheritance could be worth £50,000 or more, according to one estimate.[14] In July 2020 the Institute of Fiscal Studies said a quarter of people born in the 1980s are set to inherit £300,000 or more.[15]

The problem with inheritance

OF COURSE! ALL that money our parents and grandparents have built up in property and investments… to put it bluntly, they can't take it with them. It needs to go somewhere and it's most likely going to come down to us. But before you start measuring the curtains at Nana's country pad, hold your horses.

Yes, some of us (including me) have benefitted from grandparents handing down a bit of cash. But the average age of parental inheritance for millennials today is estimated to be 61.[16]

Just in time for our retirement, which will be a big help. But it would be unwise to depend on inheritance – particularly as 40% of millennials have never actually discussed it with their family.[17]

How do you know that a nasty shock doesn't lie in wait? That your family isn't miscalculating how much the house is worth, that the tax regime won't drastically change… that your parents haven't signed over the cash to the local cats home to teach you a lesson? (Not that Tiddles and co don't need the cash, but still.)

Besides, even if the money does come your way, how will you know what to do with it? This is particularly true for those teenagers who are starting to see their **child trust fund (CTF)** mature.

All babies born between September 2002 and 2 January 2011 were eligible for a CTF, which came with a £250 bung from the government. Family members and friends could all chip into CTFs, and the children can withdraw the money when they turn 18.

I hear of parents and grandparents who lie awake at night, worrying what will happen when their kids and grandkids reach 18 and get their hands on the money – worth five or six figures, in some cases.

If you haven't got to grips with investing, you would be completely floored by having that much money in one go. As chapter 1 showed, stuffing it all in the bank could result in your money losing value over time.

So what are you gonna do?

Just say no to YOLO*

OF COURSE, YOU could just decide to spend, spend, spend. And some young people are living it large *regardless* of how much they've got in the bank, by maxing out credit cards and overdrafts.

Some might say: "What's wrong with that? Those Brexiteer baby boomers wrecked our future and coronavirus forced us to live like hermits. We should just enjoy life, consume to our heart's content and let the future take care of itself."

C'mon guys. My time as the Young Money blogger has convinced me that we have to do better than that. I'm all for 'carpe-ing those diems', but spending every penny we have isn't a good way to do it.

Whether it's earned or given to us by others, money is precious. Once it's gone, we'd better be sure it went on stuff that really brought us joy and fulfilment.

Make your cash count!

IT'S NOT ABOUT having more cash here and now: it's what we *do* with it that counts. By learning how to invest for AND in yourself over the next 30 years, you won't have to rely on parents or grandparents handing over their wealth to you. And if that does happen, you'll actually know how to make the most of it!

It's the promise of big lump sums tomorrow that is driving companies to capture our loyalty today. And we can capitalise

---

* You only live once. Of course.

on this right away, even if the big bucks don't land in our laps for a decade or three – if at all.

We've got to start owning it whatever happens. After all, there's little point in keeping up with hustle culture, 'rising and grinding' and working your ass off to achieve your amazing ideas if you neglect the thing that could make the biggest difference to your long-term prosperity: smart investing.

So let's get down to it: what is saving, what is investing, and how are they different?

CHAPTER 3

Team Saving or Team Investing? Be both!

DELICIOUS!
The secret sauce of compounding. Adding extra spice to your money for decades to come.

IN THIS BOOK, I'm going to talk a lot about investing. Before we get into that, I want to define what I mean by investing, how this is different to saving, and why YOU need to do both.

I may have bemoaned what's happened to savings since 2008. But I am not advocating that we give up on savings altogether. I am a savings fangirl!

It's vital that every young person in the UK has short-term savings so they can avoid falling into debt. Sadly, that's not happening. More than half of all 22–29-year-olds in the UK (53%) have no savings at all.

We saw during Covid-19 just how many young Brits teeter on the edge, just one crisis away from sinking into debt. In early April 2020, soon after the first lockdown began, a quarter of under-34s had already used up their savings.[18] By July, half a million young people (18 to 24) were claiming Universal Credit or Jobseekers' Allowance, with 276,000 of them signing on since the crisis began.[19]

Don't get me wrong: what happened to young people across the UK in 2020 was not their fault. No one could have predicted that the government would stop millions of people from working.

Nonetheless, Covid-19 exposed just how fragile our finances are. Young people can only own their future when they feel secure in the here and now. Ideally, we need a combination of higher wages, lower living costs and better, timely information about debt.

But rightly or wrongly, you simply can't afford to wait for those changes to occur. The onus is on YOU to make saving happen.

Why y'all need to save

PEOPLE OFTEN THINK saving = sacrifice. It's not: saving = self-care. When you put your money in a savings account, it's still yours, just put on one side so you can access it when you really want or need it. It's so much easier, cheaper and more chilled than maxing out a credit card or dipping into your overdraft.

In chapter 1, I explained how interest rates on savings have plummeted – but it is still possible to find savings accounts that beat inflation. This isn't the main reason to save, but a bit of interest is a nice cherry on top.

Another upside of saving is that your bank or building society will always give you back your savings if you ask for them. Depending on the account you pick, this will happen either instantly, with a bit of notice or at the end of a pre-determined period (usually one, three or five years).

This is necessary for money you'll want to access sooner rather than later, whether it's to fix a broken laptop or go on that stag/hen do. There is one big exception to this rule, the cash Lifetime ISA, which we'll unpack in chapter 6.

Furthermore, your savings are protected by the Financial Services Compensation Scheme up to the value of £85,000 in case your bank gets into trouble. When picking a savings account, always check that the bank is covered under this scheme.

Time to talk about time

YOU'VE GOT TO save, and *only* save, for emergencies and shorter-term goals. Shorter-term goals are commonly defined in the financial world as being achievable within five years.

But for goals that are more than five years away, investing may be a far better choice.

Investment (noun), or invest/investing (verb), has multiple definitions and can be used in lots of different contexts. For instance, here are two broad definitions for investing provided by *Merriam-Webster*:

> to make use of for future benefits or advantages;
>
> to involve or engage, especially emotionally.[20]

But there are more specific definitions that relate to money:

> to commit (money) in order to earn a financial return;
>
> the act of putting money or effort into something to make a profit or achieve a result;
>
> the act of buying shares, bonds, property, etc. in order to make a profit.[21]

It's helpful to see that in the round, investing means the commitment of something, often money, in the hope of achieving future returns.

The key word here is commitment. Ageing bachelors might run a mile from this concept, but it's the bedrock of investing. Investing takes time. Unlike saving, your money doesn't just go (virtually) in the bank's vault, to be lent out to their borrowers for a limited time. It's out there, in the economy, doing vital stuff.

Investing means putting your cash into companies, governments, industries, assets, resources – anything that might grow your money – then waiting for that investment to come good and hopefully produce extra money for you.

There's another reason why investing is something that you do for longer than five years (some might even say a minimum of ten years) and that's **risk**. Risk runs through investing like Blackpool runs through a stick of rock. Speaking of Blackpool…

Riding the Big One

INVESTING IS OFTEN likened to going on a rollercoaster: it's an up and down kind of thang. Some investments are like those tame caterpillar rides for toddlers at your local fairground, with only very mild peril; others are like those monster rollercoasters with vertical drops and loops that would make most of us reach for the sick bag. And there's a giant spectrum in between.

But unlike rollercoasters, investments aren't built in advance, carefully designed, and safely tested to produce the exact same experience every time you ride them. Investments are unpredictable.

Unlike saving, there are no guarantees with investing. The value of investments can rise or fall at any moment due to all kinds of external factors, from a tsunami in East Asia to a new tweet from the US President (ahem). How your investments are managed – or not managed – will also play a big role.

We will explore exactly why your investments rise and fall, and how you might be able to understand and mitigate risks, throughout this book. For now, the main thing you need to know is that the rollercoaster is unavoidable.

Now with a physical rollercoaster, you always end up exactly where you started. But could the investing rollercoaster get us to a higher place – i.e. with more cash than we started with?

The past is history: tomorrow's a mystery

QUITE POSSIBLY. WE can get a sense of what *might* happen by looking at what's gone before. But we need to remember that the past is not a guarantee of what's to come.

Let's take the example of someone who was 25 in 2005. If they took the plunge and started investing £50 every month in the UK stock market that summer, they would have built up a fund worth almost £12,500 by the summer of 2020, when they hit 40. If they had managed to salt away £100 a month, the pot would have grown to just under £25,000. That's around a third more than the return from an average savings account.

Before we get too excited, I need to level with you. Many economists are predicting lower stock market returns in the future compared to the past. And the headline stats don't always tell you the whole story.

For example, the annual Barclays Equity Gilt Study is a popular yardstick for measuring the stock market's long-term potential. Its 2019 report showed that investing in shares for any five-year period since 1899 achieved a better return than savings 76% of the time. If you extend that investing period to any ten-year period, the chance of outperforming cash savings goes up to an impressive 91%.[22]

But in 2016, it was found that studies like these don't take investing costs into account and also they massage the stats by using returns from average savings accounts, rather than 'best buy' accounts which (at that time) paid much more. Naughty, naughty.[23]

If you take inflation into account, UK shares only grew about 4% a year between 1995 and 2015. That compares with about 11% a year in the previous 20 years (1975–1995).[24] Boo!

But savings rates have got worse since 2016, so even 4% would be nice to have. And if you invest smartly and keep a tight grip on costs, you could do a LOT better.

We need to learn to be okay with the uncertainty of investing. All we can confidently say is that, if the past few decades are anything to go by, taking calculated risks is the best way to grow your money in the long term. You've got to be in it to win it.

That's not because the stock market is on a constant upward trajectory. In fact, throughout your investing experience you'll see regular **corrections** – these are falls of 10% or more. According to stock market data, stock market drops of 10% occur around once every 16 months and, on average, last for 43 days.[25] All the more reason that you need to invest for the long term, so you can ride out these corrections and hopefully get back to better times.

This is illustrated in the following chart, which shows the growth of global shares in the 50 years since 1969. Yes, the path is up and to the right, but it is not a straight line – there are drops along the way.

Global shares (1969-2020)

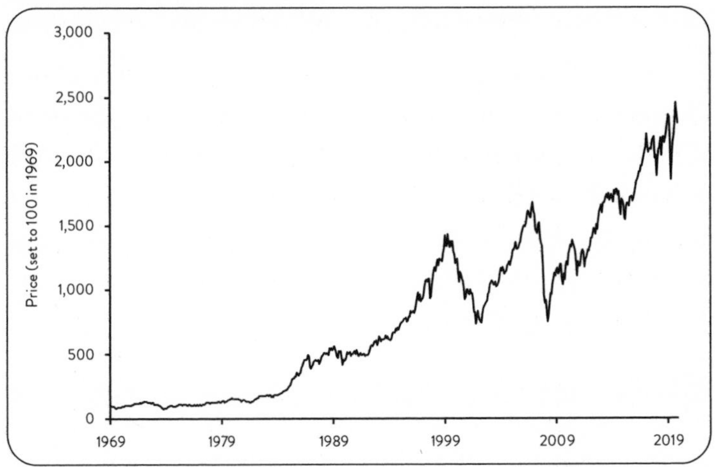

In other words, the stock market is a pretty epic engine which can drive your money harder than anything else – but only if you stay on board for at least five years. Yes, you can add more fuel as you go, and you can in theory bank some shorter-term gains if you're invested in the right way. But if you stay fully invested for longer, that powerful engine has the best chance of achieving better performance.

Compounding: the secret sauce

NOW I'M GOING to let you in on the secret sauce of investing. **Compounding** in a non-financial context means to make something that's already bad even worse. When it comes to debt, the interest you pay can attract its own interest (like a parasite) and make borrowing even more expensive.

The opposite applies to savings and investments: the returns you make spawn their own returns. And as time goes on, this builds and builds your profits.

For instance, if you invest £1000 and receive an annual return of 5%, you'll have £1050 waiting for you at the end of the first year.

But if you leave your money invested, the £1050 will not grow to £1100 after year two (as you might think), but to £1102.50, with the £50 gain from year one *generating £2.50 in its own right*. This process keeps going. Assuming constant annual returns of 5%, the same initial investment of £1000 would grow to almost £1280 after five years, £1630 after ten years and an exciting £3390 after 25 years. Yowsers!

Growth of £1000 invested at 5% annual return, after all charges

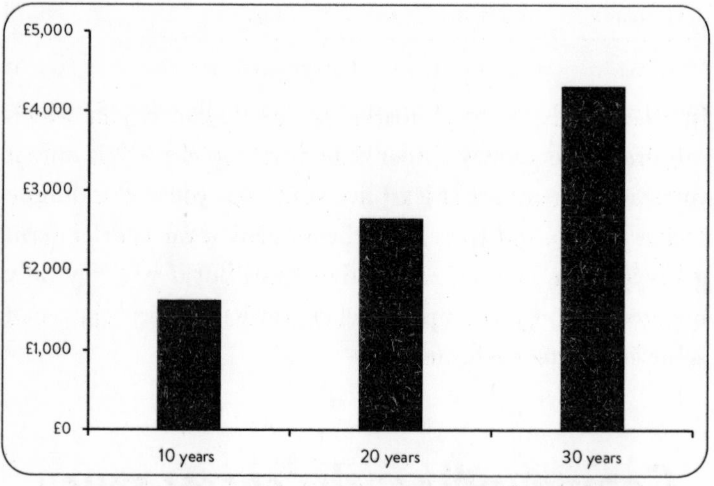

Source: AJ Bell

Of course, this principle applies to savings too, but because the returns on savings are typically lower, the compounding won't be nearly as impressive.

(Re)building the future

YOU DON'T HAVE to choose between saving and investing: you can and indeed should do both.

Saving is right for emergencies and shorter-term goals (attainable within five years) because savings are protected and can be accessed either instantly or at a predetermined time. Investing comes with no such certainty.

Investing is a much riskier, longer ride. But that's why it's *perfect* for those starting in their 20s and 30s, who have years and decades to wait for their money to grow.

Plus, we can take immense satisfaction from the very act of investing. We are committing our money in the hope of earning a financial return, yes. But investing also takes the economy forward. It helps businesses start up, grow, hire people and provide much-needed services. It helps countries and their citizens become more prosperous. It helps to fund essential infrastructure like roads, bridges, schools and hospitals. It even helps to fund new energy sources to power the world.

The politics of investing

WHAT ABOUT THOSE people who say that investing props up a corrupt world and enables immoral capitalism? That it goes against everything an idealistic young person should stand for?

This book isn't a blind defence of capitalism. It's a system with deep flaws. But even if other forms of social and economic organisation were preferable – and I'm not sure they would be – the chances of capitalism being overthrown look so slim, it would be an immense act of self-sabotage to refuse to be part of it.

Investing is an act of practical hope. It can be a tangible, meaningful way for individuals to make both their lives and the future of society a bit better. As John Steinbeck once wrote, "Now that you don't have to be perfect, you can be good."

Things are far from ideal. But anyone who shuns investing on political grounds is depriving themselves of the best chance to change things from within. As you will discover in chapters 9 and 10, idealistic young people can drive huge changes in where pension funds invest. Young people are the customers behind the meteoric rise of new financial apps that are shaking up the status quo and forcing many banks and investment companies to up their game.

By contrast, those who refuse to be part of it are not just harming their own future, but their ability to help others too. You can't pour from an empty cup. Besides, in my experience, the people who are the loudest to shout about the elitism of investing are often the ones quietly building up all their assets behindthe scenes, from high-value property to pensions. If they have decided they don't want to miss out, why should you?

The respected financial journalist Ian Cowie offers a helpful view on investing. Shareholders have tended to be better off than savers, not because the markets are automatically rigged in their favour. They invest in the companies that produce the goods and services we use every day and so they're likely to "benefit from improvements in efficiency and inventions that occur over time." He goes on:[26]

> By contrast, depositors [savers] do not buy a stake in these businesses, but instead settle for guarantees they will be paid interest and get their money back. Unfortunately, those guarantees can prove illusory, for when inflation is running higher than the rate of interest paid by most savings, the

> only certainty that cash really provides is the certainty of getting poorer slowly.
>
> One of the most important things they don't teach you at school is that a capitalist society in effect gives everyone a choice: you can either work for money or you can make money work for you.

Ian's right. You can either plod on, overworked and underpaid, waiting for others to make things better for you. Or you can take charge of your money and decide your own destiny. I prefer option 2 – don't you?

Now, you might be pumping your fist in the air, thinking: "YES! I want to know more."

Well, hang on a sec. I'm loving the enthusiasm, but it's essential that you build a solid foundation for your money before you take things to the next level. Let's find out: are you ready to invest?

CHAPTER 4

The essential beginners' checklist

BASED ON EVERYTHING we've looked at so far, I completely understand why more and more young people want to get started with investing. The number of 20- and 30-somethings using a stocks and shares ISA (which I explain in chapter 20) has jumped by 90% in recent years.[27] We don't want to be left behind!

But sometimes, it feels like young investors want to do the financial equivalent of a Tough Mudder, complete with electric shocks and ice pools, before they can even walk. I have seen smart young professionals pour their hard-earned cash into cryptocurrencies they barely understand and into risky investments marketed as safe savings.

It doesn't help that the financial industry and government often push young people towards complex financial products without addressing the basics. For example, millions of people are being automatically enrolled in workplace pension schemes when they don't even have a penny in savings (we'll dive into pensions in chapter 7).

Before you can use all the knowledge I share in this book, it's crucial you get to grips with the fundamentals of personal finance. Because you want to own this stuff too, right?

Just a caveat: this is by no means an exhaustive guide to the fundamentals of personal finance. That's for another book –

and happily, I have already written that one! (You can still buy my first book, *Spare Change*, as an e-book on Amazon.)

I also recommend you seek out all the resources I include in the checklist below. On we go…

Have you tamed costly debts?

This encompasses:

- Overdrafts.
- Credit and store cards.
- Guarantor, personal and/or payday loans.
- Debt owed on buy now, pay later schemes.

You need to get these debts under control before you consider investing.

Student debt is a bit different. It's only deducted from your pay when you earn above a certain amount and will get written off after 30 years anyway.

For consistently high-earning graduates (particularly those on new higher interest rates), paying off student debt might be a good idea. I recommend checking out MoneySavingExpert's thorough guide to student loans, as the rules vary depending on your circumstances.[28]

You also don't want to throw the baby out with the bathwater. Not all debt is bad, though there's a lot you shouldn't touch with a bargepole. Some debt can help you achieve goals (like getting a mortgage to buy a house) that would otherwise be more difficult.

Low-level, stable debt could help you maintain a decent credit score that will allow you to borrow cheaply for certain worthwhile goals. I suggest reading up on how to do this smartly: the Money Advice Service has a helpful guide.[29]

You should NEVER go into investing if you are struggling with debt and you should NEVER invest to try and pay off existing debts.

Are you bossing your budget?

DO YOU KNOW how much money comes into your bank account every week or every month? Do you keep an eye on what you spend? Do you consciously think about what's good value for money?

If not, don't worry – you're just not in the budgeting zone (yet). But there are plenty of apps that will get you there. You can choose a budgeting app that will assess your incomings and outgoings if you're happy to stick with your main bank, like Money Dashboard, Emma, Yolt, Plum or Chip.

Alternatively, you can switch to a digital-first bank like Monzo or Starling to see your spending in real-time – which can come as a BIT of a shock – and totted up in different categories.

The aim is to achieve a good balance between your earning, spending, saving, donating and investing. That's budgeting in a nutshell. Schedule a few sessions a week to look over your finances and see what could be improved.

Can you pay for all your essentials?

THIS IS A biggie. There will be lots of young people who will always struggle to achieve this, no matter how carefully they budget. I don't know if you are one of them. You'll have to honestly decide whether you are already making the best of what you've got. But if I had to pick three essentials everyone can nail, they would be:

- keeping a handle on food costs by cooking more, having homemade lunches/coffees and saying "Bye, Felicia!" to takeaways,
- making sure you're on the best mobile deal available (ideally SIM-only rather than needlessly pricey contracts) and…
- avoiding 'show and throw' – that is, repeatedly showing your card to card readers and thus throwing your money away. Get a special pre-paid card, load it with the money you can afford to spend on days/nights out and only take that card out with you.

Do you have money left over at the end of each month?

IF NOT, THEN you can't save and invest. Once you start budgeting and paying less for your essentials, you need to reach the point where you're spending less than you earn. This usually means having a little (or maybe big!) think about your discretionary spending – i.e. anything that isn't strictly necessary.

We all need to check in with our spending and figure out if it could be smarter. Even small changes can make us feel far calmer and more in control.

Have you got an emergency savings pot?

IF NOT, GO and set one up. Now. Do it, seriously.

You could open an easy access account with a savings provider – try to pick one that offers the best interest, they're easy to find in so-called best-buy tables online. Or you could use 'savings pots' that allow you to round up the spare change from your shopping. That means when you spend £3.70, 30p automatically goes into your savings pot.

Off you go! I'll be here when you get back, don't worry…

Done it? Brilliant. Now think about HOW you're going to save (if you're not going to rely on round-up savings, that is). Can you set up a direct debit for a certain amount to go into your bank account when you get paid? If so, think of it as paying your Future Self first. Are you going to put any unexpected bonuses, tax rebates or that cash bung from Nana in there? Of course you are.

Some savings are better than no savings, but if you're looking to invest, you're advised to have at least three months' worth of your salary in your easy access pot. If you don't have it yet, save until you do.

Do you have insurance for your income?

THIS IS OFTEN the last piece of the money puzzle that young people forget, or don't even know exists. But without it, the whole financial jigsaw would crumble in a matter of weeks if you lost your job, fell ill (mentally or physically), or had a serious accident. It happens so much more than you think. And unfortunately, statutory sick pay is not very much (just under £95 a week, as of 2020) and is only paid out for 28 weeks.

The good news is that you can get insurance that will cover your income or give you a decent payout if the worst happens, but may in any event offer all kinds of sweet perks while you stay in good health. Make sure you contact a trusted independent broker, like Lifesearch or Drewberry Insurance, who can help you find the right policy.

The best is yet to come

I'VE THROWN A lot at you there. I appreciate you might not have ALL that stuff completely down pat. Maybe some of it is a work in progress (I won't tell anyone).

In the meantime, stick with me as I explain what exactly is going on with your finances and how they interact with the economy, our society and the whole planet.

My job here is to help you understand that while spending and saving mindfully can give you a great start in your adult life, it's just that. The start.

The rest – and the best – is yet to come. But before we get stuck into investing proper, I notice there's a rather large, ungainly elephant sitting in the corner of the room, refusing to budge.

That elephant is housing. And you might be wondering what the hell to do about it. Maybe you're stuck in rented accommodation, fed up with your landlord and wondering whether you'll ever be able to get the keys to your first home.

Increasingly, young people are turning to investing to try and make those keys magically appear. Are they right?

CHAPTER 5

Should I buy property?

THESE NEXT TWO chapters are going to be for those who have not yet bought a house or are unsure about doing it. If you have bought one (go you!) or you *know* for whatever reason that these chapters are not relevant, feel free to skip them and go straight to chapter 7.

So far, we have examined why it makes sense to save *and* invest. And hopefully by now, you're starting to understand which #lifegoals lend themselves more to investing – really long-term stuff that's decades away – and which ones are more suited to saving: going on holiday, paying for a wedding, getting that tattoo that will make Mum cry…

"But Iona – where does property fit into all this?" you may be thinking.

Gosh. You're asking a big question there. In this country, we're *obsessed* with housing, from buying it and improving it to selling it for a fat profit.

And millennials are not exempt from this fixation. Surveys consistently show that most young people still prefer to own property rather than rent. Yet those same surveys also show that young people feel increasingly gloomy about their chances of ever buying their own home.

This book is not primarily about our byzantine housing market. We're talking about how to own our future through investments.

But many young people will view their home as the biggest investment they'll ever make, with some justification.

Let's look at the arguments for and against home ownership as a valid aspiration for young people in the UK today.

Let's rehabilitate renting

FIRSTLY, THERE IS ZERO shame in renting. Our society shouldn't ever make young renters feel inferior to homeowners. Renting is a perfectly smart choice for anybody who is still finding their feet and deciding what they want from life, or those who harbour doubts about settling down at the first opportunity.

That's because renters can move around more easily than homeowners if they need or want to. They don't have to take responsibility for repairs or renovations. They can live in pricey areas that could enhance their career prospects and quality of life in the short term.

Besides, nearly all of us will have no choice but to rent at some point. Students have to do it at university. Others will find it's a better option for their career, privacy and sanity, compared to living at home with their family.

Plus, taking out a mortgage is a BIG commitment. You should only do it when you are good and ready. Being mortgage-ready involves:

- Building up your credit rating over time and getting your finances on an even keel to get approved for the mortgage you need.
- Having enough money to pay for your deposit plus survey and legal costs.

- Becoming relatively settled in your career so you know you can afford the monthly mortgage payments and various bills.
- Wanting to live in a specific area for a decent period.

Let's say you tick these boxes, either now or in the not-too-distant future. Does buying still make more financial sense than renting?

This is a vexed question. The answer depends on where you buy and the direction of both property values and rental costs in that area. Unsurprisingly, there are lots of conflicting conclusions online, usually coming from sources that use superficial data and have a vested commercial interest.

What does independent academic research say? One study published in 2019 looked at the pure financial returns of home ownership for first-time buyers in the UK from 1975 to 2011. Researchers from the Edinburgh Business School at Heriot-Watt University looked at historical regional and market data like rents, house prices for first-time buyers, mortgage interest rates and loan-to-value ratios.

Mortgage speak

WOAH! I JUST threw some nerd-talk at you. Let's break things down before we look at that study. The **loan-to-value ratio (LTV)** is what mortgages are made of: it tells you how much you'll need to raise for a **deposit** (the percentage of a property's value that you need to pay upfront) versus what your bank/building society will lend you. A 95% LTV mortgage means you'll have to cough up 5% of the property's value as a deposit, with your bank lending you 95%.

The higher the deposit you can raise, the lower the **interest rate** you'll pay on the mortgage. Mortgages, remember, are a type of debt and therefore you'll be paying back what you owe, plus the old **APR** on top, over the **term** of the mortgage (typically 25–30 years, but up to 40).

If you're a first-time buyer, you (or your mortgage broker) can find mortgages with lower interest rates if you save up for that bigger deposit. Even a 10% deposit (to get a 90% LTV mortgage) will make a big difference compared to a 5% deposit.

If you have a larger deposit, it will reduce your chances of getting into **negative equity**. This occurs if house prices drop significantly after you buy, meaning your mortgage debt is more than the market value of your house. This makes it difficult to sell your home or **remortgage**, aka move to a new mortgage when your existing deal ends or find a cheaper deal.

Anyway – back to that study I mentioned, which spanned 37 years and three major housing cycles.[30]

Renting vs ownership: the verdict

THE STUDY FOUND that the average first-time buyer who bought a home in 1975 and sold it in 2011 created 12.4p of wealth for every £1 they initially spent on their deposit.

The researchers also calculated the average return *per year* of ownership, as not all would have owned the same home for 37 years! That led to the finding that each year, first-time buyers typically generated an extra 61p for every £1 spent on the initial outlay (e.g. the deposit). So, over a decade, you're getting £6.10 per initial £1 spent.

This requires further research, but the data does suggest that first-time buyers needed just two years to regain their initial investment. Okay, this wealth doesn't translate into extra money in your bank account straightaway. But, like an investment, it builds up over time in the form of money saved as you pay down your mortgage and, eventually, the amount you make from selling your home.

Now, you may be thinking: "Ah, but we're talking about a crazy time in British history when our parents bought sprawling mansions for £5 and their value rocketed, so they're now sitting on goldmines. That may never happen again."

That's a fair point – but research found that growth in house prices contributed 56% of overall financial returns for homeowners. The rest was made up of other benefits, such as building up equity and enjoying lower housing costs as the mortgage gradually reduced: something that is never possible with renting.

Yes, property wealth in some areas was more down to rising house prices, less in others. But every single region saw homeowners enjoying greater overall housing wealth compared to renting.

I don't include this research to make you feel rotten if you are still renting. But perhaps it is comforting to know that a simmering ambition to buy your own home isn't a sign you have been brainwashed by your elders. It's a sign that you understand how the UK housing market works.

Thanks to tortuous planning laws and a slug-like rate of housebuilding, we have a shortage of good-quality homes in desirable and promising areas. That means people who can buy those homes and keep them in good condition will find generally that the investment at least maintains its value in the long term.

Of course, there are no dead certs. It's hard to predict what will happen to house prices in any given neighbourhood or region in the future. These are influenced by myriad factors, both national and local.

Also, the Edinburgh study found that those who bought property at the peak of a housing boom typically saw a far lower financial return than those who made the same decision just after a housing slump. It pays to understand what stage we might be at in the housing cycle so you can time your property purchase well.

And where are we now? Following the temporary cut in stamp duty by the chancellor in July 2020, prices were not expected to fall much in 2020, despite an impending recession. But forecasters warned that a property crash could be delayed until 2021, with the CEBR predicting a house price fall of over 10%.[31]

Help to Buy: buyer beware!

THERE ARE SOME SERIOUS pitfalls you need to avoid as well. More than 200,000 people in the UK have bought a home using the Help to Buy Equity Loan scheme, which was launched by the government in April 2013.

Under this scheme, the government (or should we say the taxpayer!) lends you 20% of a property's value, except in London, where it's 40%. The maximum property value allowed is £600,000, which means you could be borrowing as much as £120,000–£240,000.[32]

You then only need to save up for a deposit worth 5% for a mortgage worth 75%. You won't be charged fees on the government loan for the first five years, but the idea is that you'll be able to start paying back this cash thereafter.

Sounds fantastic! And it has been – for a small number of big housebuilding companies. That's because you can only buy a new-build home from one of the handful of firms signed up to the scheme. It has put rocket boosters under their profits and helped them to monopolise the homebuilding market. They have been provided with "an almost endless source of state-financed, captured and slightly desperate buyers", says Merryn Somerset Webb, editor of the financial magazine *MoneyWeek*.[33] Help to Buy purchasers may pay anywhere between 5 to 22% more than people buying newbuilds outside the scheme.[34]

That's not all. You'll have to start paying back the interest on those loans, which is 1.75% in the first year before rising in accordance with the **Retail Prices Index (RPI)**.

The average rate on the loan is 5.2% – way higher than what you typically pay on today's mortgages. To cap it all, you must pay back the government a percentage of the value of the house when you come to sell it.

If you borrowed 20% to buy a home worth £200,000–£400,000, you have to pay back that same percentage of the sale value. If your gaff is now worth £400,000, £80,000 goes back to the government (not including the interest). So you not only risk making an initial overpayment that leaves you in negative equity on the traditional part of your mortgage, but also that you don't have enough equity to move up the ladder when the value of your house goes up and you have to pay back your loan.

A further scandal in new-build housing erupted after the Grenfell Tower fire in 2017, in which 72 people died. It transpired that combustible cladding of the kind that fuelled the fire had been applied to thousands of other high-rise buildings in the UK.

The cost of removing this cladding will be around £3bn, most of which is falling on leaseholders unlucky enough to live in these buildings. They face bills worth tens of thousands of pounds and a nightmarishly long wait for the removal process and paperwork that would allow them to sell their properties or re-mortgage. According to the End Our Cladding Scandal campaign, 1.5 million flats are in this ruinous (not to mention dangerous) situation. The tragedy also brutally exposed lax regulation of homebuilding standards and a broken system where high land values and bonuses for meeting fast deadlines reward "shoddy workmanship and finishing quickly", according to one fire safety expert.[35]

Home truths

THE BOTTOM LINE is that home ownership is a perfectly valid aspiration – but not at any cost. If you're thinking about buying under the Help to Buy Equity Loan scheme, I strongly urge you to think again. It's far better to wait a bit longer and save a bit harder until you have built the full deposit you need so you can choose a property on the open market, free of all these crappy conditions. You've also got to be clear-eyed about new-builds that look shiny and high-spec but may come with expensive structural flaws, thanks to poor standards of housebuilding in recent times.

Otherwise, buying a home should be as much a personal decision as a financial one. Your house isn't just an investment; it's a home. The financial journalist Liam Halligan has written:[36]

> Owner occupancy has given millions of ordinary working people a chance to accumulate wealth, build a tangible stake in the economy, gain more control over their lives

> and leave money to their children. There are also proven positive links between owner-occupancy and participation in community organisations and broader civic engagement, with ownership speaking to a visceral human instinct.

I bought my first home in my early 20s, partly thanks to money passed down by my late grandmas (thank you, Romany and Joan). It wasn't a mansion, but an ex-local authority property in an 'up and coming' part of London with surely the grottiest bathroom in the postcode.

But it's one of the best decisions I've ever made. Having a stable home in London has given me a real professional edge. And once I paid down my mortgage (during what I call the 'baked bean years'), I was able to plough more cash into other long-term investments.

And this is crucial. A recent study from the Investing and Savings Alliance found that lifetime renters will need an additional £9,000 of income per year to cover rental costs compared to homeowners – meaning they will have to save nearly twice as much into their private pension.[37]

To cap it all, once you own a home you can decorate, renovate and titivate exactly as you see fit, with no landlord to tell you off if you break their rules. Not only did I finally get that new bathroom I longed for, I've been also able to indulge my taste in chinoiserie wallpaper. You can't put a price on that, folks.

If you are itching to put YOUR stamp on a home, you've found an area you really like with a promising future, and you can envisage being able to pay off a mortgage for the kind of home you want, the next question you may be asking is: should I save or invest to build up a deposit?

CHAPTER 6

Should you save or invest for your first home?

Investing means putting your cash into companies, governments, industries, assets, resources – anything that might grow your money – then waiting for that investment to come good and hopefully produce extra money for you.

There's another reason why investing is something that you do for longer than five years (some might even say a minimum of ten years) and that's risk. Risk runs through investing like Blackpool runs through a stick of rock. Speaking of Blackpool…

Riding the Big One

INVESTING IS OFTEN likened to going on a rollercoaster: it's an up and down kind of thang. Some investments are like those tame caterpillar rides for toddlers at your local fairground, with only very mild peril; others are like those monster rollercoasters with vertical drops and loops that would make most of us reach for the sick bag. And there's a giant spectrum in between.

But unlike rollercoasters, investments aren't built in advance, carefully designed and safely tested to produce the exact same experience every time you ride them. Investments are unpredictable.

Unlike saving, there are no guarantees with investing. The value of investments can rise or fall at any moment due to all kinds of external factors, from a tsunami in East Asia to a new tweet from the US President (ahem). How your investments are managed – or not managed – will also play a big role.

We will explore exactly why your investments rise and fall and how you might be able to understand and mitigate risks throughout this book. For now, the main thing you need to know is that the rollercoaster is unavoidable.

OKAY, IF CHAPTER 5 has reassured you that buying a home is still a worthwhile #lifegoal (if done smartly and for the right reasons), then let's think about how you're going to build that almighty deposit. If the whole housing convo is not relevant to you, you can jump to the next chapter.

In years gone by, there was only one recommended route for wannabe buyers: that was to stick to saving – no ifs, no buts.[38]

That's because it's widely assumed that most first-time buyers are aiming – and able – to get those keys within five years.

This surely rules out investing for your first home, right? As we saw in chapter 3, investing is only suitable for goals that are more than five years away.

Well, not necessarily. High rents and subdued wage growth have meant that many young people have needed to save for much longer than five years to get on the property ladder. In fact, that waiting game has typically been ten years across the UK, rising to 15 years in London, according to research from Hamptons International.[39]

And something else has changed the rules of the game too. It's called the Lifetime ISA (LISA). I mentioned it in chapter 3 as one of the exceptions to the barren savings rule right now. And boy, what an exception it is too…

First, let's get to know the ISA family.

Meet the ISAs

ISA IS AN acronym, standing for **Individual Savings Account**. It's a legal structure that was launched by the government in 1999 and it allows anyone to save into it, up to a certain amount, and hold any interest or investment returns they make within it tax free. Everyone gets an **ISA allowance** each tax year, which begins on the 6 April, and right now it's £20,000 a year (though this can change).

You can put your allowance into one or a combination of ISAs: there are currently four available for those aged 18 and over. One has closed to new customers (**Help to Buy ISA**) and another can only be opened for someone under 18 (**Junior ISA**). Remember that the ISA itself is not a product but a tax-free 'wrapper' for your cash or investments.

We'll get to know the three other key members of the ISA family later. Let's concentrate on the latest addition: the **Lifetime ISA**. Launched in 2017 by the government, it can only be opened by someone aged 18–40 and it can be used either for your retirement savings or to buy your first home. For now, we'll focus on the latter.

The LISA is the first vehicle that provides a real incentive for young people to invest for their first home. That's because there are two different versions of the LISA and both come with a bonus from the government. You can either put your LISA into cash or you can put it into investments through what is commonly described as a stocks and shares LISA.

Every £1 you put into the LISA will be topped up by 25p by the government. The maximum you can save into a LISA annually is £4000 – so that means you could get up to £1000 free cash towards your first home every year. If you saved the full whack allowed from the minimum age of 18 to the maximum age of 40, you could get £32,000 free from the government. Blimey!

The cash version of the LISA offers interest in addition to the government bonus, which varies depending on the provider you choose. The rates haven't been stellar – the best I have seen so far is 1.5% – but the government bonus is effectively a 25% interest rate anyway, making the cash LISA the most lucrative savings vehicle out there by a LONG way.

Cash vs stocks and shares

THE STOCKS AND shares LISA is, potentially, on another level. As we saw in chapter 3, equities do tend to outperform savings over longer periods.

So, the possibility of much better returns may well tempt you to invest for your first home. But I'm about to slap some huge health warnings on this strategy.

Firstly, remember that the past really is no indicator of the future. Yes, research shows that investing in shares outperformed cash in most five- and ten-year periods *historically*. But will this happen again in the future?

Secondly, the performance of your stocks and shares LISA will depend on where and how it is invested. There isn't one single investment you can buy that will magically do the job. In part 2, we will explore how having a carefully chosen buffet of investments – known as a **portfolio** – can reduce the risks involved (without ever being able to remove risk completely).

Which brings me on to my last, most important point. What happens if that stock market rollercoaster plummets and shows no sign of rising again for a good while? Uh-oh.

You might have to wait months or even years for your investments to regain their value. That's the last thing you want when you've had your fill of renting, or you've found the right place at the right price, and you need to pony up the cash for your deposit straightaway.

Young people who were on the cusp of converting their stocks and shares LISA into a first home deposit early in 2020 had to think again when stock markets crashed due to Covid-19.

So that presents a conundrum. Should you open a stocks and shares LISA to invest for your first home? Here are the main questions you need to ask yourself.

The key LISA questions

Are you sure you want to buy?

THE LISA IS by far your best bet if you're 100% certain you want to buy property. But if you change your mind, you'll pay a 25% penalty on any withdrawals from the LISA, which claws back the government bonus and takes some of YOUR money in the process too.

Note that this 25% penalty was temporarily cut to 20% following Covid-19. Many people were unable to access Universal Credit – the main benefit offered by the government – because their LISA savings counted against them. This penalty cut is still in place at time of writing, with pressure from many advocates (including me) to maintain it after the crisis passes. But the current plan is to reinstate the 25% penalty at a later stage.

In the meantime, I recommend that you only take out a LISA if you can commit to it. Otherwise, you need to find other savings accounts that will pay an above-average rate of interest.

Are you confident that you will buy within five years?

If so, there is no point thinking about investing – stick to your cash LISA.

How comfortable do you feel risking your home deposit?

This is a toughie. Yes, a stocks and shares LISA can and should be invested in a way that will reduce your risks, which is particularly important when you're relying on this money to fund your first home. But ultimately, if you can't stomach the idea of your money being at any kind of risk whatsoever, it's best to play it safe.

When people are new to investing, they often overestimate how much risk they are willing to entertain because it's tricky for them to accurately predict how they will react if markets fall.

Of course, you can get a LOT more comfortable with risk when you learn more about investing.

But if you think there's *any* chance that a fall in your investments would freak you out, and possibly provoke you to withdraw your money, it's vital that you listen to that instinct and go with a cash LISA. Nobody knows your mind better than you.

Don't hang your hopes on housing

HERE'S MY FINAL word on the whole housing shebang before we move on. If you're still renting, please do read the rest of this book. It's just as much for you as anyone because all young people need to get to grips with long-term saving and investing, regardless of their housing status.

Buying a home isn't compulsory and neither is investing towards a home deposit. It's totally fine to choose to save for your first home in a cash LISA, or even in a regular savings account, if you're not sure. In fact, it might be the best thing to do if you're looking to buy within five or ten years and you really don't feel comfortable taking that extra risk.

Most crucially, you shouldn't put all your faith in housing. Yes, it's lovely to have a place you can call your own, but don't get *too* comfortable in your new crib. Your financial journey is far from over.

If you can achieve your home-buying dream, you have a fantastic opportunity to open new financial horizons. The temptation might be to sit back, hope that house prices will grow and rely on selling your property one day for big bucks, perhaps to fund your eventual retirement. After all, that seems to be what a lot of boomers are doing (or at least *claiming* to do…).

But that would be a big mistake. Personal and professional reasons should be behind your home-buying zeal as much as financial ones. Besides, property should only be one part of the plan to build your long-term wealth. And when it comes to your later life, there is one product I've touched on earlier but am now about to blow wide open – your pension.

Not least because you're probably already saving into a pension! Didn't you know? Oops, sorry to break it to you so suddenly.

It's about time you got to know what a pension is and what YOU need to do to ensure you have a fabulous later life.

CHAPTER 7

Time to mention your pension

RIGHT – LET'S get one thing straight. I HATE the word 'pension'. I dare say you're not a big fan either. When I hear it, I think of that road sign warning motorists to slow down for 'elderly people', featuring two sad figures hunched over – one with a walking stick (of course).

I also think of pottering, gardening, eating mashed-up food and watching daytime TV. Nothing wrong with any of those things (I have been known to do all four), but they don't really give pensions that sexy, dynamic vibe that makes young people go: "Yea! Bring it on."

And let's face it, all those activities I mentioned are the more benign (if crudely stereotypical!) stuff commonly associated with being old. What about the negative aspects of ageing, like ill health, loneliness and death? It's that stuff that makes people fear their later life and deters them from making plans for it.

It doesn't help that it feels like a LONG way in the future. Combine that with the fact that nobody really talks to young people about their pensions in an informed and balanced way, and it's no wonder that most of us put the p-word on the back burner.

Yet the idea behind a pension should be simple and empowering. Most of us don't want to work forever. So why not save throughout your life so you build up enough money to – one day – stop or at least cut back your work, and do something else with your life?

Let's try the f-word instead

KINDA LIKE A **future fund**, rather than a pension – amirite?

For some people, their advancing years might look like the traditional 'retirement' I described before, filled with gentle errands. For others, it might be a bit more exotic, with trips abroad, or perhaps more adventurous, with physical activities like cycling.

Some might prefer to keep on working, but at a more relaxed pace or on a different kind of project. And others might relish getting more active in the community, volunteering for charity, or helping friends and family. My dream retirement, in case you're curious, would be a blend of *all* these options.

Now, you may think to yourself: "I don't ever want to retire – I *love* my work." That's wonderful, but let's see if you feel that way in another 30 years. My dad loved his journalism job so much, he said he would do it for free. But the minute he turned 65, he was OUTTA there!

None of us know what the future holds, and we humans aren't great at predicting how we'll think and feel further down the road. So, it makes sense to keep your options open. And building up your pension – sorry, future fund – gives you more choices further down the line.

Alas, most young people I know don't see it this way. When they do think about their pension (which is very rarely), they tend to see it as a problem, not an opportunity. Pensions now come with a ton of historical and political baggage – most of it negative. A lot of young people say to me that they'll never get to retire, and even if they do, there won't be a pension for them to fall back on.

Things won't be nearly as bad as that (especially if more people read this book and act!). But there is a grain of truth in their analysis.

A short history of pensions

PENSIONS HAVE BEEN around since 1908. They were introduced by then-Chancellor David Lloyd George in what he described as a "great experiment":

> You have never had a scheme of this kind tried in a great country like ours, with its thronging millions, with its rooted complexities …

Pensions used to be funded mostly by the government and (later on) employers when life expectancy was lower and people's retirements were relatively short. For example, the first pension in 1908 was only paid at the age of 70: at that time, just a quarter of the population lived that long and life expectancy beyond 70 was typically just nine years.

Since then, we've come a long way in public health, from the creation of the National Health Service and childhood vaccinations to vast improvements in how we treat cancer, strokes and heart attacks. This means the average retirement is lasting longer than ever – and that is creating a proper headache for employers, the government and individuals alike.

Times have changed since our parents and grandparents joined the workforce. They tended to receive generous pensions from their employers. These were known as **final salary** or **defined benefit (DB)** schemes and, as their name suggested, they provided a guaranteed income linked to the final salary earned just before retirement. All your parents/grandparents needed to do to get this pension was to keep working and stay alive.

Baby boomers have also been (for the most part) fortunate enough to receive the most generous state pension in British history. In 2011, the then coalition government, comprised of senior Conservative and Liberal Democrat politicians, rustled up a policy designed to appeal to their older voters known as the 'triple lock'. This promised to keep raising the state pension by 2.5%, the rate of inflation or average earnings growth, whichever figure was the highest in each year.

The triple lock is still in place (at time of writing), even though most pension experts don't believe it is sustainable. The cynical part of me suspects it's because governments prefer bribing groups more likely to vote for them in the short term over doing what's best for society in the long run. No wonder that this generation of pensioners has recently been found to have, for the first time in history, a higher average disposable income than those still in full-time work.[40]

Look, I don't blame today's pensioners. They worked hard throughout their lives and went through their own tough times (as I point out in chapter 1). It's also worth stressing that as many as two million pensioners still live in poverty, a problem that may have actually got worse over the past five years.[41] But the consensus is that young people today will have to take far more responsibility for building their own future fund than was previously the case.

Bye-bye DB, hello DC

PRIVATE EMPLOYERS ARE increasingly closing final salary schemes to younger employees amid fears that they are proving un-fundable as we live longer (though public sector workers still get a bumper deal).

So DB pensions are becoming rarer than photos of Kim Kardashian wearing a jumper. And the chances of *our* state pension retaining the triple lock are as high as Kim dropping a new cozy thermals range.

The majority of younger people (at least in the private sector) will have to settle for a **defined contribution (DC)** deal. With this pension, there are no guarantees on the benefit you will get when you retire. With a DC pension, the amount you pay in – the contribution – is defined, but not what you will receive in payments when you retire.

Hang on a moment though. I mentioned at the end of the last chapter that you are probably *already* in a pension. How come that's the case? And surely that means you're well on the way to building your future fund? Well, let me explain something called auto enrolment.

Automatic for the people

AUTO ENROLMENT WAS introduced in 2012 and saw every full-time worker in the UK aged over 22[42] earning over £10,000 put into a pension, provided by their employer. A percentage of your salary is deducted 'at source' – i.e. as soon as you are paid – and diverted into the pension fund. Your employer will also put some of their money into the fund.

It's not compulsory to stay. You can opt out. If you do that, you won't be re-enrolled for another three years. But most people's default position will be to do sweet FA.

If you keep saving into the scheme, you'll be building your future fund all the way through your career, meaning you won't be reliant on the state pension in that (potentially) long last chapter of your life.

The good news is that auto enrolment ensures that most of us are saving *something* for retirement, even if we don't fully know it. Now for the bad news…

There's evidence that auto enrolment may have *reduced* the amount that employers put into workplace pensions. As recently as 2016, employers were paying on average 17% of salaries into DB pensions and the employee was paying 5%. But since auto enrolment was rolled out across the workforce, employees now typically pay in 5% (with 1% tax relief) and the employer just 3%.[43]

That makes a total pre-tax contribution rate, for most people today, of 8%. At least it's taken out of your pay before tax, so you get the full benefit. But unfortunately, if you want to enjoy the kind of retirement that smug Auntie Maureen has been enjoying, with cruises to Antigua and a suspiciously youthful visage, the pension wonks reckon you need to be saving a LOT more.

The exact figure depends on when you start and how much you want to retire on. Some have suggested that if you earn an average salary of £27,000 and want a 'moderate' standard of retirement, you need to put away the grand sum of £800 a month over your whole working life (or £753 a month for a couple, who can share costs more easily **so need to save less**). This works out at about 25% of your earnings.[44]

And here's a scary warning from the World Economic Forum. Han Yik, head of the WEF's Institutional Investors Industry, says:[45]

> The real risk people need to manage when investing in their future is the **risk of outliving their retirement savings**. As people are living longer, they must ensure they have enough retirement funds to last them through their longer lives. This requires investing with a long-term mindset earlier in life to increase total savings later on.

The WEF would like to see pension funds across the world design more adventurous default funds – i.e. ones invested in riskier assets to generate better returns – to give younger people a bigger head start. Otherwise, our pension pots won't grow enough for our later years and we'll have to rely on the state pension and selling some Harry and Meghan wedding gewgaws we might have knocking around in the attic.

The scariest part is that most of us are blissfully unaware of this impending crisis: a third of workers don't even know they are automatically enrolled,[46] while fewer still understand that they are probably not contributing enough to have a banging retirement. Separate research shows that more than a fifth of 18–34-year-olds are in low-risk pension funds.[47] Even when young people *do* grasp the situation, most have no idea how to tackle it.

Why you should stay in

AT THIS POINT, you may be thinking: "You're asking me to put 25% of my salary into a pension?! Iona, are you out of your tiny mind?"

Trust me, I get it. I have been telling the pensions industry for a while that high contribution targets can be unrealistic, demoralising, and counterproductive. They might cause some people to go: "Sod it. I need all the cash I can get. If what I'm putting into my workplace pension won't amount to a hill of beans, I might as well opt out."

Please don't. That would be a real doofus move. The question you should be asking is not: "Can I afford to stay in my pension?" but: "Can I afford *not* to?"

Let me explain why it usually pays to stay in your company pension.

The money is automatically deducted 'at source' – so you can't really miss it

If you earn £27,000 (the UK average salary), you can expect to pay £73 a month into a workplace pension. But under the pay-as-you-earn system (PAYE), the money is deducted straightaway when you are paid. While you might have appreciated that extra cash for the here and now, you don't have to make the active choice to invest it for retirement instead. The decision is taken for you – and since it is usually the right one, it's one less thing to worry about.

You're getting free money from the government – and your employer

As a minimum, you pay in 4% of your salary – but your employer pays in 3% of your gross earnings too. And then the government tops it up with tax relief which adds another 1%.

What the hell is **tax relief**? Basically, it allows you to save tax that you would have paid on your earnings by diverting the money into a pension. If you are a basic-rate taxpayer and contribute £100 from your salary into your pension, the amount paid into your pension is actually £125. That's because the government adds an extra £25, paying you back the £25 it took in tax on that £125.

By starting early, you can get a much better fund in retirement

If you've opted into your workplace pension early in your career, you *should* see your future fund grow over time due to two factors.

Firstly, it will be invested in the stock market, which has historically produced better returns over most timeframes than cash, though bear in mind all the caveats mentioned before.

You should hopefully be starting to understand that the longer you can invest, the more risk you can take. By definition, your pension is going to be invested for a long time – until you retire, which is many decades away.

Secondly, don't forget the secret sauce of compound interest, mentioned in chapter 3, where your returns attract their own returns. Tasty!

No silver bullet

IF ALL THIS is surprising – you have a pension, who knew? – it should also be reassuring. It shows you are already invested in the stock market.

We still have some way to go before we can confidently say we're owning it, but it shows investing is less scary and remote than you might think.

Auto enrolment is a neat idea. Starting a pension, future fund, kickass retirement kitty, whatever you want to call it, might otherwise be a daunting and unappealing piece of life admin. But a large part of the decision has been made for you by auto enrolment. If you stay opted in, you can benefit from the three amigos of long-term investing: compound interest; tax relief from the government; and free money from your employer.

That said, auto enrolment is no silver bullet. It is an extremely blunt tool, designed to help most people have *something* rather than *nothing* in retirement. There are many people being left out of auto enrolment, most notably the self-employed, who need to come up with a Plan B.

And even if you are part of the auto enrolment action, it won't automatically create the later life fund that you deserve – or indeed the kind of future society you want to see – unless you get involved.

CHAPTER 8

Solutions to your pension problems

AUTO ENROLMENT MAY seem like a refreshing exception to the rule that, if we want to upgrade our finances, we should get off our backsides and actually *do* something.

However, while staying opted into your workplace pension is an easy win for most, it should just be the start of your later-life plan. Relying on auto enrolment is, pension-wise, the equivalent of livin' on a prayer – and as legendary as Jon Bon Jovi is, I wouldn't advise taking his lyrics as your financial credo.

So here's how to hack your way to a better future fund – one that might make even loaded Auntie Maureen a tad envious.

Before we get stuck in, I should stress that pensions aren't the simplest of things and as you get older (and near that dream retirement age), the decisions you make become more complicated and more important. If you have any questions about your own personal situation, you should DEFINITELY seek out professional financial advice. Otherwise, let's get problem-solving!

PROBLEM: The contributions you're making could be higher

A WORKER IN a private company can typically expect 8% of their pre-tax salary to be automatically funnelled into a pension.

But experts unanimously agree that we should try to save more. The figure I have seen cited most often is 12%, though this would also include the employer and tax contributions. How do you know if that's the right level for you and the lifestyle you want?[48]

The solution: You can make extra contributions above the minimum level. Even better, see if your employer will offer **contribution matching**. If so, they will give you even more free money if you can save more into your workplace pension. If your employer offers this, bite their hand off!

By way of illustration, an employee aged 25 on average earnings could boost their pension pot by £43,900 at state pension age if they increased their contribution by just 1% above minimum contribution rates and this was matched by an additional 1% from their employer (making a 10% total contribution). This assumes wage growth of 3% and investment growth of 4.25% after charges.[49]

Extra pension value at age 65 with extra 4% contribution

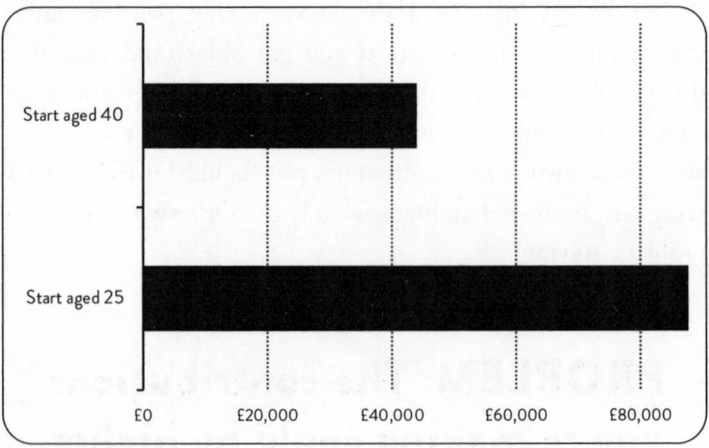

Source: Aegon

Also, I recommend checking out the Retirement Living Standards by the Pensions and Lifetime Savings Association.[50] This groundbreaking initiative gives you a concrete idea of how much you would need to save to achieve a 'minimum', 'moderate', or 'comfortable' lifestyle, based on the real cost of goods and services you would be typically buying in each tier.

The website gives the example of 'Rosa', who's 25 years old and earning £31,892. If she sticks to the default contribution of 8%, with £8,500 in her pot so far, she would likely only have an annual retirement income of £16,678 – putting her in the 'minimum' tier, where she could afford a £38 food budget and coach holidays in the UK. But if she increased total contributions to 12% – or £106 extra a month – she could enjoy a higher weekly food budget, more eating out and holidays abroad.

This is a useful way to see past the terrifyingly high contribution targets thrown out there by experts *assuming* we want safaris abroad and a new kitchen every 10 years in retirement à la Aunty Maureen. Maybe we do, maybe we don't. The point is you can decide for yourself, then save accordingly.

Also, don't beat yourself up if you can't save the optimal sums straightaway, perhaps because you're prioritising other goals like your first home. It's always good to have a target to work towards. And as soon as you get a pay rise or a bonus, or achieve another financial goal, make a pledge to put any extra cash you have freed up into your pension. Your future self will love you long time.

You can also open a **private pension** (also known as a **personal pension**). These are offered by private companies and operate in a similar way to workplace pensions. There is no employer contribution, but you still get tax relief and you can find a much wider choice of investments.

You may also come across stakeholder pensions – these were introduced around 15 years ago as a way of capping fees on previously expensive pensions. But the charge cap of 1.5% actually looks very high these days: make sure any charges you pay are a lot lower.

PROBLEM: The self-employed and part-time workers don't get this deal

PEOPLE WHO ARE self-employed for tax purposes are not automatically enrolled into pensions. However, you might be auto enrolled into a client's pension scheme if you earn above £10,000 a year working for them. That's because you may have been classed as a worker under employment law, which requires companies to automatically enrol you.

This is one scenario where opting out might be a smart move: small patches of auto enrolment here and there will not necessarily work very well for the self-employed and gig workers, due to reasons I flag up later in this chapter.

The solution: You can open a private pension for yourself. The government sets a cap on how much people can contribute to get full tax relief: the lifetime allowance is about £1.7m (at time of writing) with an annual cap of £40,000 – more than enough for most people!

You can also join **NEST – the National Employment Savings Trust**. It's a pension scheme that was set up by the government after auto enrolment to ensure all employers, even the smallest, have an affordable but well-managed pension scheme.

Another option right now for the self-employed is the LISA. I mentioned it as a powerful vehicle for first-time buyers in chapter 6, but it's also possible to use it for your retirement. You can get up to £1000 a year free from the government, which is akin to the employer's contribution you're otherwise missing out on, if you save the maximum of £4000 a year until you are 50.

You then wait until 60 to access the fund completely tax free. Early withdrawals are penalised, but possible if necessary (and free if you're terminally ill). The LISA offers more flexibility than a pension, particularly in retirement, but the maximum of £5000 a year, even with investment returns added in, may not add up to a very substantial fund when you retire, so you should use a private pension or NEST as well.

PROBLEM: You can't access your pension until you're 55

THERE ARE A few exceptions to this rule, like if you're terminally ill or work in professions that often necessitate early retirement, such as sport. Though something tells me David Beckham doesn't need his pension early.

Pensions are designed to be long-term funds that must be left alone to grow in the stock market. But that leaves many feeling under the cosh. What if you have financial problems and could really do with the cash now?

The solution: Obviously, the solution is NOT to accept the offers of those slimy salesmen to access your pension early.

Lots of pension boffs might say: "Iona, shut up. This isn't a problem – it's a great thing." The fact is that our pension is locked up until 55 for our own good, so it is ready for us when we need it.

But there is some force to the argument that the big lock-up is problematic for those on lower incomes, struggling to save or invest for more immediate goals. To help combat this, NEST has teamed up with various employers to experiment with a so-called **sidecar savings** scheme (think of Wallace and Gromit, aww).[51]

This pioneering trial allows workers to automatically build a savings pot from their earnings. Once they hit their savings targets, they put the extra monthly contributions towards their pension pot. They can then withdraw the money from their sidecar savings if they need it and start the process again.

This scheme looks promising so far and could hopefully be rolled out nationally in the future. In the meantime, create your own savings sidecar and put this money in an account you can access in a jiffy.

PROBLEM: Your pension doesn't move with you

TODAY'S YOUNG WORKERS will typically have multiple jobs throughout their life, moving in and out of full-time employment more than ever before. That means they will leave behind lots of different pensions with different employers. Neither you nor your employer will contribute any more to the pension once it's left behind – but fund managers will still be taking a charge.

These fees will eat into your micro-pots, thus diminishing their worth when you come to retire. Plus, we're liable to forget about all these pots over the course of our careers.

The solution: The government and pensions industry are working together to come up with a so-called **pensions dashboard**. This would be an online hub that allows you to see all your pensions in one place, possibly with a view to transferring all those pensions into one pot quickly and easily. It's not ready yet; nor is it guaranteed to include every pension out there. It will be a big step forward though – watch this space.

You can transfer your pensions into one pot yourself, but it's always best to take financial advice if you're curious about this option, as you might not be best placed to judge which pension is best to transfer the others into. However, if you have a series of relatively straightforward DC pensions (as opposed to more complicated DB pensions), you could do a lot worse than use an app like PensionBee to consolidate all of them into a single online plan.

A work in progress

PENSIONS AIN'T PERFECT – not by a long shot. From their origins as a "great experiment" way back in 1909 right up to the present day, pensions have and always will be a work in progress. Even now with the advent of auto enrolment, the system still gives a significant (some might say unfair) advantage to those in the public sector, at major companies who can afford to pay higher contributions and those with access to better-paid, full-time work.

Then there's the UK's shocking gender pension gap. By the time a woman reaches 65, her pension pot will typically be worth just a fifth of a man's, according to the Chartered Insurance Institute.[52] Divorced women, meanwhile, typically end up with a pension worth around £26,100, compared to £103,500 for divorced men.[53] Clearly, something is going badly wrong.

Earnings and pension values for men and women

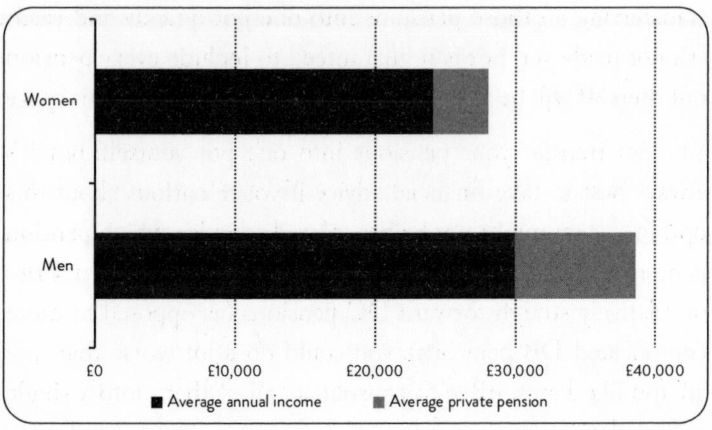

Source: NOW Pensions

The problem is that women miss out on building up their workplace pension because they take more time out of their jobs to look after children or elderly parents than men. They are also more likely to work part-time and not qualify for workplace pensions, earn less and make lower contributions or rely on their partner's pension, which usually leaves them much worse off should they divorce.

But ladies, you CAN do something about it!

In this chapter (and the last), we majored on the extra steps you can take to beef up that fund, which can be summarised as:

- Staying in your workplace pensions if you're a full-time employee.
- Starting an additional private pension (and possibly LISA) to boost your retirement fund.

- Starting a private or NEST pension, with a flexible LISA top-up, if you're self-employed.
- Staying on top of all your pensions throughout your working life.
- Saving more into your future funds whenever you can.

Pensions will continue to reign as the dominant way to invest for later life. Because of this, pension funds – and the ordinary folks like you and me invested in them – wield extraordinary power and influence.

The question is: are we using that power for good?

CHAPTER 9

Could your pension save the world?

WHO WOULD HAVE thought that a Scandi teen could spearhead a global movement? That's exactly what happened in 2018, when Greta Thunberg renewed the international debate on climate change. Her solo protests outside the Swedish parliament soon led to a worldwide campaign, calling on governments to cut emissions and invest in greener infrastructure.

We can all take action to reduce our carbon footprint. Perhaps the single most transformative thing we can do is change how we invest.

Our workplace pensions in the UK are worth more than £2.6 trillion.[54] They invest in businesses, create jobs, fund projects from hospitals to railways, and back energy sources that fuel the world. Gives a whole new meaning to the idea of a *future fund*, no?

But few of us seem to grasp this amazing fact. A survey of 2000 people in 2019 suggested only a quarter of 18–34-year-olds understand that their pensions are invested in the stock market, which in turn affects the economy and climate in a very real way.[55]

TBF, pension funds have been lousy at communicating with us. Once a year, they send reams of docs in the post (very eco-friendly!) stuffed with geek-speak. If we can be bothered to read this stuff, it leaves us feeling more confused than before.

No wonder so few of us realise we are investing in the world through our pensions. And fewer still are able to identify any shortcomings of the funds we are invested in, ethical or otherwise.

Think of me as your investing Greta (minus the pigtails) as I open your eyes up to what's REALLY going on.

Default duds

WHEN WE ARE automatically enrolled in a workplace pension scheme, we are put into a **default fund**. As the name suggests, it's the default option that most of us stay in until we leave the company or retire.

The truth is that the default fund is not the only game in town. Your workplace pension usually comes with a range of funds and you can choose to switch away from the default and invest elsewhere.

"Why would I do that?" you might think. "I haven't got time to think about all those other options. Surely the big guys are taking care of things and making sure the default is good enough?"

Oh, your faith is touching! Yes, default funds are fine. Sort of. Just about. Maybe. Well, err, not always.

Granted, they are relatively low cost because there is a charge cap on pension funds, currently set at 0.75% of your money each year. Fees matter an awful lot because the higher they are, the lower your overall returns will be. We will look more at the killer impact of fees later.

Default funds also play on the safer side, so you can be reassured your money isn't being put into stupidly risky endeavours like, say, prospecting for gold on Mars. So that's something.

But there's major room for improvement. Firstly, it's a lottery: in 2019, it was revealed how investors in the best-performing default funds enjoyed returns that were four times higher than those in the worst-performing funds in the previous five years.[56]

Okay, these sums are academic right now because pension funds are supposed to be invested for decades to come. Some do better one year, others do better the next. What happens in one five-year block is not too significant. Overall, the returns of the different funds could balance out in the long run. Even so, it's fair to say some default funds could be doing a lot better.

Secondly, default funds could be behind the times on important stuff like climate change and social responsibility too.

Woke-up call

THE JAPANESE NOVELIST Haruki Murakami once wrote: "Everyone, deep in their hearts, is waiting for the end of the world to come." Everyone, it seems, except young people.

Research, news reports and my own experience suggests millennials and Gen Z (roughly denoting today's teenagers and early 20-somethings) are more determined to protect the future of the planet than anyone else. Most of us – 62% – want to make a positive difference in the world. And 88% of us feel more motivated in jobs where we can work on social and environmental issues.[57]

I have a hunch that you're not overjoyed by the idea of your money being invested in companies that make weapons or mass porn, promote gambling, dodge tax, exploit workers, undermine society and local communities, harm our health or degrade the environment. Me neither.

But in 2018, a report by the campaigning organisation Share Action found that's exactly what most of the 12 biggest pension providers in the UK were investing in.[58] Only two had specific policies to challenge companies on aggressive tax avoidance. Only three excluded investments linked to chemical and biological weapons. One wasn't even making sure it avoided investments in landmines and cluster bombs. Only a handful of providers had analysed the carbon intensity of their default funds, let alone taken any action.

Just one provider stood out for having a thoroughly ethical approach to investing. NEST, already mentioned in previous chapters, was the only provider at that time prepared to seriously address what Share Action described as "climate-related financial risks". I'll explain what that means later, but first, let's get into the concept of **ethical investing**.

Historically, ethical investing has been a niche pursuit. Only a minority of funds have barred dubious companies (known in the industry as **negative screening**), let alone actively sought out the good eggs.

There has been a longstanding perception that ethical investors make less money because they automatically sacrifice the juicy returns that come with 'sin stocks' like tobacco, oil and alcohol companies. The thinking was that only a committed (and slightly mad) goodie-two-shoes would put morality ahead of more moolah.

It hasn't helped that there has been a morass of confusion around what ethical investing is. For starters, it isn't always called ethical investing: some call it **impact investing**, others call it **socially responsible investing**. And what does it even mean to invest ethically? Are your ethics the same as my ethics? Can an investment ever be completely ethical? If it can't, then what should we prioritise?

The O.G. of ESG

THESE WILL NEVER stop being contentious and fascinating issues. But there are now three words that are commonly used to define ethical or responsible investing. These are:

- **Environmental** – this covers carbon emissions, water stress, climate change, pollution, waste and renewable energy.
- **Social** – this relates to the rights, well-being and interests of citizens and their local communities. This takes in privacy and data, workers' rights, supply chains (including use of overseas sweat shops) and health and safety.
- **Governance** – this focuses on how businesses are run, looking at issues like board and employee diversity, tax transparency, anti-competitive practices, accountability and so-called 'fat cat' bosses on excessive salaries.

Together, these create the acronym **ESG**. This term has exploded in popularity in recent years and has catapulted the concept of ethical/responsible/impact investing to the forefront of finance.

Today, it means much more than just negatively screening out the rogues. It's about engaging with companies directly and talking to their leaders about how to improve the way they do business.

That's because there's a growing belief that companies which behave badly or produce dangerous products come with their own risks – not the good kind.

Take tobacco. Once one of the world's most consumed products, in 2019 it was removed from the investments of NEST due to what it described as "stricter worldwide regulation against tobacco products, increasingly aggressive legal action by governments … and falling global smoking rates." Mark Fawcett, NEST's chief investment officer, said:

> In our opinion, tobacco is a struggling industry which is being regulated out of existence. We have not taken this decision lightly but we don't think it makes sense to continue investing in an industry whose business model looks increasingly unsustainable.

That last word is pivotal. Investors are increasingly trying to suss out whether certain businesses are *sustainable*, in all senses of the word.

We can't say for certain if tobacco is finished. Companies in the sector are still posting fat profits, not least because they are shifting into vaping and even legalised cannabis – again, a wonderfully progressive move or an immoral step backwards, depending on your POV.

But it's clearly wise to question whether certain industries really have a sustainable future and if not, whether we should be asking them to change their strategy or pull out our investments altogether.

Fossil fuels may have seemed like a logical investment in a previous era when they were indisputably our main sources of energy and their carbon emissions were either poorly understood or ignored out of convenience. That era is over. The Paris Agreement in 2015 saw countries across the world commit to reducing their greenhouse gas emissions to net zero by 2050.

That's why NEST was a real O.G.* by addressing "climate-related financial risks" before anyone else. NEST argued that traditional oil and gas companies would come under huge political and civic pressure in years to come, potentially denting their profits, and adjusted its investing approach accordingly.

---

* That's Original Gangster. Oh yea.

Covid-19 has given new impetus to the existing debate over fossil fuel investments and has cast a long shadow over the aviation and travel industries, as long-term investors think harder about a sustainable economy.[59]

Callous companies are also increasingly unacceptable to wider society. In 2020, the miner Rio Tinto caused international outrage when it destroyed an ancient 46,000-year-old sacred Indigenous site in Australia to expand an iron ore mine. Its CEO and two senior executives were forced to resign after coming under major pressure from Australian pension funds, with the scandal likely to increase regulation of mining operations in historically or environmentally important regions in the long run.

Today, we've all got to figure out whether our money is backing the right horses. But if only it were that simple!

Working at the greenwash

IN OCTOBER 2019, the UK government introduced new rules forcing pension companies to place ESG at the heart of their investment decisions. That's progress, right?

Dig a bit deeper, however, and you'll find that many funds adopt a strategy they cryptically call **best in class**. These funds don't exclude any industries, but invest in individual companies that seem to meet ESG rules.

Is this a fudge, a way to game the system? It certainly leads to some curious decisions. Some funds invest in defence giants on the basis they treat their workers well. Others stick with oil and gas companies because they talk a big game when it comes to cutting emissions, even if they're still lobbying governments to water down eco-reforms. And some regard tech giants as the good guys, while their transnational tax dodging goes under the radar.

Pension funds all too often rely on impressive-looking reports produced by companies keen to tick lots of virtuous boxes. No matter if the underlying business destroys natural habitats or props up corrupt regimes; if it recycles all its office paper and has a float at a Pride carnival, it's in!

Okay, I exaggerate – but only slightly. The truth is that the only funds that truly tally with most people's idea of ethical investing are impact funds. Impact investing is the most considered form of ethical or responsible investing, whereby you only seek out companies that demonstrate a purely positive social impact. But I'll be surprised if impact funds become routinely available to workplace pension investors anytime soon.

For pension funds, the only way is ESG. And that may mean being fobbed off with a fund designed to score highly in the ESG game, but which may have found a few cheat codes thanks to some highly paid consultants along the way!

As things stand, default pension funds won't be winning woke prizes anytime soon. At time of writing, most still own shares in BP and Royal Dutch Shell. Others own shares in Nestlé, which comes with a long list of scandals, while Facebook also crops up despite concerns over its tax practices, data handling and how Mark Zuckerberg seems to be the unelected king of the world.

Time to follow through

CLEARLY THE VERDICT on most pension funds would have to be "must try harder". But in their defence, this stuff isn't easy to get right.

For example, research[60] has shown that even the companies running stock market indices and **ratings agencies** (which rate the financial viability of companies and even governments) disagree violently on whether a firm is ESG friendly. One rates Tesla, the 'clean' energy empire run by Elon Musk, as top dog for sustainability; another believes it to be the world's worst car producer.

Neither are necessarily wrong. They just look at different data. These are complex judgements in a world where things are rarely black and white.

And if pension funds must try harder, the same goes for all of us. Yes, more and more of us are *saying* we want to save the world – but do we really mean it?

It's time to put your money where your mouth is!

CHAPTER 10

Woke up your workplace pension

OKAY, SO WE'VE seen how pension funds may not be living up to our most virtuous expectations. But we also need to take a long, hard look in the mirror (the selfie mode on your phone doesn't count) and ask if we're doing enough ourselves.

Barely a week goes by when I don't hear about a new survey suggesting most millennials care, like, SO deeply about where their money is invested. Among investors aged 25 to 34, some 53% go for sustainable funds, while only 28% of those over 65 do the same – or so the Schroders Global Investor Study from 2018 claimed.

If that's true, why aren't sustainable funds bigger? The International Monetary Fund estimates there are now more than 1,500 equity funds with an "explicit sustainability mandate". These funds control nearly $600 billion in assets, three times the level in 2010. But they still represent less than 2% of the total fund world.[61]

Now I know that baby boomers have more money than millennials, but still. Something's not right. Indeed, a 2018 survey found millennials are twice as likely as over-45s to believe it is their responsibility to ensure their pension is invested ethically. But still, only 13% of them actually took action.[62]

Aha. Some honesty, at last! How can we turn things around and put words into action?

The vice of virtue signalling

FIRSTLY, WE NEED to disregard surveys that portray millennials as more activist than they really are. Researchers go to young people and ask: "Would you like your money to be responsibly invested?" And we say: "Yea, of course!"

Nobody in their right mind would say: "Nah, use my money to murder hedgehogs and torch forests, for all I care."

I'd *like* my money to be responsibly invested, just as I'd *like* to have dinner with Tom Hardy. But that's not the same as making it happen, is it?

Unlike landing a date with an A-lister, it's not *that* hard to move your money into responsible investments. Most pension schemes today do offer ethical funds. They're not perfect, but they're more ethical by most people's standards than the default.

Why do only a tiny minority of us make the switch? Well, it's no bother to sign an online petition, fire off an angry tweet or pop to town for a disco-dancing protest. Changing how your pension is invested is less obvious and requires a teeny bit more thought.

"Give me a break, Iona!" you might be thinking. "I'm trying my best, but I had no idea about all this until now." That's fair enough. After all, how many pension funds really talk to us in a way we can understand?

That's why we need an accurate picture of the number of millennials who invest 'ethically'. Only then will we start to grapple with the very real barriers faced by young people trying to behave responsibly.

Moreover, it becomes harder for investment funds to get away with the kind of greenwashing we highlighted in the last chapter, to coast on a wave of smugness, knowing they've aced the public relations but faced no real scrutiny.

Educate yo-self

PENSION FUNDS NEED to be dragged into the 21st century in the way they communicate. Right now, they send out letters (and sometimes email, if they're a bit groovier!) that are so badly designed and written, they're either ignored or cause bewilderment.

Hardly any talk about the fascinating and important stuff we've uncovered in these chapters – where's the sense in that?

Share Action has called on firms to invest in apps, snazzy video content and social media.[63] Others believe those letters (known as **annual statements**) should be revamped.

Consultancy Quiet Room, law firm Eversheds Sutherland and pensions supremo Ruston Smith have come up with a much better template with simple language and colour-coded sections that fits nicely on two pages and can be read in less than two minutes. That's what I'm talking about!![64]

The government is also considering making envelopes orange and forcing companies to send them out at the same time to create a national statement season, with such ploys working well in Sweden.[65]

Which brings us back to Greta. If she can be nominated for the Nobel Peace Prize (twice) before she is legally old enough to drink, I'm *pretty sure* you can move some of your pension money into more ethical funds.

Here are your next steps.

Log on to your online pension account

That's a good start! You can find the details in the welcome pack you got when you were enrolled. Alternatively, search your work email or ask your employer. You may have more than one pension if you've worked for more than one company, so look these up too – you can use the Pension Tracing Service[66] if you've mislaid the info.

Research your pension fund's investments

Your pension account should tell you what fund you're in. But don't expect it to give you a full rundown of the companies it invests in. Funds usually only release their top ten holdings and even those aren't always publicly available. Grrr.

Some funds might list their investments on their website, so go there first. Start by searching terms like "investments" or "fund factsheet" and you should find their annual report. If the fund lists an index like the FTSE 100, you can easily look up all the holdings online. You could also try emailing or calling your pension provider, or ask your employer to do it on your behalf.

Check out the ethical option (if it's there)

Your pension provider should clearly list the alternatives to the default funds. But they may come with odd names and scant info, so make a note of them and research them online.

There should be at least one fund that's ethical. There should also be one or more funds that will take greater risks than the default for those investing for the long term. With some providers, you can switch in minutes during your lunch break, but others require you to make a call or write an email. Check out their FAQs or help section.

Your pension is most likely to be in something called a **mastertrust,** a type of pension that had to be set up when auto enrolment was introduced. That means there is a high chance that you will be able to move into a fund that's more aligned with your values and risk appetite (NEST, The People's Pension and Standard Life Mastertrust are all on board with this agenda).

Many bigger companies already offer **group personal pensions**, which are also easy to switch if you're in a defined contribution scheme. However, if you are in a defined benefit arrangement, switching is almost certainly a bad idea. Hang in there – DB schemes are rapidly improving their approach to ESG – and look for ethical choices through your private pension and LISA instead.

Suss out your red lines

You may decide the ethical option, while not flawless, is a damn sight better than the default. You also need to weigh up whether the ethical option is taking enough risk for the time that you will be invested in the stock market and what the costs are.

Don't feel guilty about taking that other stuff just as seriously as ethics. An international survey from 2019 found young investors aged between 23 and 35 in the UK, France, Germany, Australia, Hong Kong and the US insisted that when it comes to investing, there are three things that matter more than anything: returns on capital, low fees and transparency.[67]

Even when it comes to ethics, some things will matter to you more than others. You will almost certainly have to compromise, but I think it's better to achieve small but real change than do nothing to preserve glorious ideals.

Take action

If you're looking for more systemic change, you've got to channel your inner Greta. Contact your employer. Write to your MP. Speak to your professional union. Talk to your colleagues. Go forth and remember what Miss T says: no one is too small to make a difference.

BONUS CHAPTER

Could (and should) you retire early?

BEFORE WE MOVE on to part 2, there's one more thing we need to consider: the FIRE movement. It started in the US and has gained quite a following in recent times. It seems to be revolutionising how millennials live, work and manage their finances.

What is FIRE? And could it work for you?

Many of us dream of ducking the 9-to-5 and living a more liberated lifestyle. You may feel trapped by your current situation and wonder if you'll ever be able to escape it. And maybe you've come across FIRE already and either think: "Retiring early sounds brilliant, tell me more" or "Yeesh, those influencers are hardcore. It's not for me."

Either way, stay with me as I demystify the FIRE movement – not least because it's a fascinating insight into the kinds of choices now possible with modern investing. It may just inspire you to think a bit differently about what you want out of life.

Getting all FIRE'd up

FIRE STANDS FOR 'financial independence, retire early'. Okay, it's grammatically crude, but you get the picture.

It's about cutting your spending to the bone so you can save and invest as much of your disposable income as possible.

Ideally, you also devise some canny ruses so you can earn money without working for The Man, like hosting affiliate advertising on a website or social media page (known as **passive income**).

Hey presto! You create a big enough fund so you can quit your job, live off the proceeds and do whatever your heart desires – travel the world, bring up a family, write weird erotic thrillers.

To paraphrase Shakespeare: "Why then, the world's mine oyster, which I with investing and passive income will open." The whole thing sounds like a dream come true – at least at first glance. Let's give it the once-over.

Let's do the math

THE MAIN THRUST of the FIRE movement is to build up a pot of money at least 25 times the amount you'd ideally like to live off each year. For example, if you want an income of (say) £40,000 a year, you will need to have a FIRE pot of £1 million (25 x £40,000). I think I need to lie down in a cold, dark room…

FIRE experts love to *Do The Math* (say it in an American accent) and they've pinpointed 25 as the golden number. It's based on the 4% rule: that you withdraw no more than 4% of your retirement fund each year so you never run out of cash.

How much money do you need to invest each year to reach that goal?

It depends on how soon you want to 'retire', how much you earn and what your income needs to be when you no longer work. But the most common figure bandied about is that you need to save between 50–70% of your salary.

No, that's not a misprint, you read that correctly.

Some FIRE experts disagree that you need to save that much, saying 20–25% of your annual income is sufficient IF you start early enough and IF you achieve nice 'n' healthy returns on your investments. That's quite a few ifs!

How the hell do you manage this feat? First, you dramatically reduce your spending. That means meticulous food planning – zero takeaways or lattes – trading down to basic products, and replacing holidays and nights out with cheap or free activities. That's a lot of baked beans and tap water, then. And you'll have to do this for years, too.

Finally, you put most of the money you've saved into the stock market, specifically through passive investments like **exchanged-traded funds (ETFs)**.

This is an increasingly popular investing strategy for young people, whether they're FIRE-mad or not. The two main reasons are that they are relatively simple to trade and cheap. I will explain more about how they work in part 2. ETFs have a lot going for them, but you should keep an open mind about what kind of investing strategy to adopt as you read the rest of this book.

Infuriating as well as inspiring

MANY FIRE INFLUENCERS paint ETFs (so many acronyms!) as a straightforward yellow brick road to massive investment returns, financial independence, and the life of Riley.

The reality is more complicated. Much of the FIRE movement has been predicated on rising stock markets, particularly in the US, over the past decade. But what happens if the stock market doesn't perform as well in the future as it has in the past?

That may not be a problem if you're genuinely investing for the long term, as historic evidence suggests shares and bonds get their mojo back if you give them time. But if the clock is ticking down to an arbitrary early retirement date and your investments are under the weather, you probably shouldn't tell your boss to take a hike just yet.

Millions of millennials are performing miracles just to invest 10% – let alone half – of their salary each month. And the things that FIRE advocates deem an outrageous waste of money… don't they make life worth living? That cold beer with friends on a summer's day; unforgettable nights at a concert or the cinema; that lovely meal with close family. Covid-19 and the ensuing lockdowns have been a painful separation from those experiences.

FIRE is not for everyone. Typical FIRE followers are male, techy types who love calculating compound interest, many of whom are already very privileged and enjoy lots of financial advantages over low earners. And it's ironic that many haven't actually retired early, but have just shifted into monetising blogs, vlogs and courses on… how to retire early! The revolution will surely eat itself.

How Covid-19 changed things

HOWEVER, THERE IS something profound to take away from FIRE – especially post-Covid. Most of us work long, rigid hours for a fixed salary, determined by someone else, only to fritter it away in tiny slithers of spare time. Why?

The media, our education system, often well-intentioned families, all prime young people to believe that a high-earning job is essential if they want to be secure and happy. But too often, we end up spending nearly all we earn – egged on by large commercial interests – as a consolation prize for the exhausting, stressful demands of full-time work.

We buy stuff that rarely brings lasting fulfilment, and that we are too stressed and time-poor to appreciate anyway. We also end up paying the convenience premium, where we come to rely on expensive crutches (like takeaways) to make our working lives easier. Then there's lifestyle creep, where we become more high maintenance each time our income rises, and we increasingly view luxuries as essentials.

Covid-19 broke that relentless work-spend treadmill. We had time out from the huge coffee 'n' commute expenses associated with office-based working.

At the same time, lockdowns completely shut off our usual spending avenues. Some of the daily savings demanded by FIRE that once seemed absurd suddenly became doable. That's why credit card debts were paid off and savings increased in record amounts during 2020.

Redefining work

DON'T GET ME wrong: many people are well suited to the structure of full-time work, especially when they have a vocation. A good thing too, because many critical jobs will always require dedicated people on call. And it's entirely possible for employees to maintain work-life balance and reject lifestyle creep, though not without enlightened employers and a big dollop of self-discipline.

While working is not the be-all and end-all, most of us would feel lost without it. What matters is how we define 'work'. For some, only the cut and thrust of a corporate job will do. For others, it's more about creative projects, social activism and looking after others. Plus, Covid-19 demonstrated all kinds of jobs, around which we build our whole lives, can suddenly become 'unviable' due to events outside our control.

Pre-Covid, experts like Lynda Gratton and Andrew J. Scott from the London Business School were arguing the conventional three-stage life – education, full-time work, complete retirement – is becoming extinct due to the rise of artificial intelligence and greater longevity. Even if the changes we'll see may not be quite as dramatic, it's definitely time for young people to consider the bigger picture.

In my view, that means thinking beyond traditional pensions. As vital as they are, they shouldn't take up all our long-term financial bandwidth, which is why the financial industry's obsession with them can seem a bit out of touch. We need to be much more flexible and open-minded when thinking about the future and how we plan for it.

When I was a full-time employee earlier in my career, my spending was higher than it is now I'm a freelancer, even though I'm earning more. Why? I'm older and wiser, but also more fulfilled and connected to my income, since I now produce it entirely on my own through creative, purpose-driven work.

This has allowed me to create space for saving and investing, which then frees me up to choose higher-quality work, do nice stuff with my family and pursue passion projects – like this book!

I don't think we should all be aiming to retire at 40 – that's an unnecessary and pressurising target. Besides, studies have shown humans have an innate need for work that solves real problems or moves society forward.[68]

What we can do is think much more deeply about what we want out of life and whether early investing can help us achieve it. That's gotta be worth something, right?

A future to feel good about

BESIDES BUYING YOUR own home or enjoying a nice retirement, you may have all kinds of aspirations swirling around in your mind. Maybe it's setting up a business, becoming a full-time creative or getting married. The orthodoxy is that you should start breaking down those goals and working out how far away they are and how much they would cost so you can make your investment plans.

The problem is you can't map out your life in exact detail, especially when you're young and still finding your way in the world. Nor would you want to. Happiness is surely a harmonious mix of savouring the moment and working towards meaningful goals.

No one would deny that goals aren't important. I just think the financial industry (and yes, some FIRE influencers) get so hung up on the need to crystallise all life goals as a prerequisite for investing, they end up alienating a lot of young investors who are still figuring out what they want.

Fixating too much on future goals can become unhealthy. I'm a recovering goal-aholic, having spent much of my young life measuring my self-worth by what I accomplished. So much of modern society pushes us to prioritise materialistic over spiritual gains. That's not a recipe for happiness.

Nonetheless, I invest because I have dreams. And Gloria Steinem once wrote that dreaming is a form of planning. I am planning for events, needs and opportunities in my life that may never happen, but if they do, will make me glad to have money on standby. It's about being forward-looking, not forward-obsessing. As I've said, investing is an act of practical hope, so the more positive and optimistic we are about our future (and indeed the future of the world), the more we'll want to invest in it.

So, we need to keep working on our personal growth, alongside learning about investing, to ensure we feel good about life and have goals in the future that are genuinely right for *us* – not just conceived to impress our parents or generate likes online. Don't worry, I'm not about to recommend a barrage of cheesy self-help books. Just listen to your instincts, follow your heart and, once you've made your plan – and committed to that dream – stick with it.

PART 2

How do we Own It?

IN PART 1, we went deep on the importance of investing, blasted through the basics of saving and investing, made short work of the two big p-words (property and pensions) and even unravelled how to invest your way to a better future.

Part 2 is where we get down to business and explain the how of investing. You may have lots of unanswered questions by now: where do I go to invest? What do I need to know? Should I buy shares in Amazon? Is Gary from work really a millionaire because he buys Bitcoin? And what the hell should I do when something like Covid-19 tears the markets a new one?

Fear not! In part 2, I will:

- Unpack the digital revolution in finance and how to navigate this exciting but complex new world.
- Explain why funds are such a massive part of investing, then look at whether you should go active or passive.
- Delve into robo-advice (sorry, nothing to do with Robocop) and whether it could work for you.
- Analyse the new breed of trading apps and why you should be clear-eyed about the millennial-baiting companies they promote, like Facebook and Amazon.
- Give you the lowdown on Bitcoin, P2P, crowdfunding and minibonds, then lay out all the different asset classes, from equities to commodities.

- Go into what it takes to manage your own investments, from picking a strategy to keeping an eye on costs.
- Give you the tools to deal with spivvy influencers and head-turning trends.
- Let you have a peek of my investor diary as I report on my own efforts to deal with the most recent market downturn amid Coronavirus.

Without further ado, let's look at where your investing journey will most likely begin: that incredible super-computer in your pocket. How did we get to the point where we could own our financial futures simply at the tap of a screen?

CHAPTER 11

The evolution of investing

AH, THE SMARTPHONE. What would we do without it? Since the iconic iPhone 4 came into our lives in 2010, tech has reshaped the way we live, with Brits now typically checking their phones every 12 minutes.[69]

The younger generations are especially plugged into the online world – perhaps worryingly so.

Is our love-hate relationship with smartphones going to become just hate? Is it obliterating our focus, narrowing our horizons, putting us in permanent short-term mode? After all, social media companies employ techniques usually associated with casinos, like 'pull-to-refresh' buttons that mimic slot machine levers, to get us hooked on their products.[70]

Surely this is a bad thing – especially for our finances, which require us to think sharp, for the long term and certainly not with a gambler's mentality!

But if technology is the source of so many problems, it's usually the place to start seeking solutions too. Yes, digital life is messy, nasty, even dangerous. But it can also lead to more knowledge, convenience and choice.

Nowhere are the opportunities – and hazards – of tech more apparent than in our finances.

Exciting investing opportunities now come onto our radar all the time, from the chance to buy shares in brands we love with a few taps, to the promotion of forex trading and crypto currencies through Instagram.

Technology has made the once elite pursuit of investing available to pretty much everyone. But, as Uncle Ben told Peter Parker (in *Spiderman*), with great power comes great responsibility. It requires us to understand how online investing works and, more importantly, how to make it work for *us*.

Let's start by looking at the history of investing technology. I'm about to introduce a lot of key concepts and phenomena that will feature throughout part 2. Strap in!

Big Bang theory

THERE HAVE BEEN several waves of technological innovation in modern finance. Arguably, the first big breakthrough occurred in the 1980s, when Prime Minister Margaret Thatcher deregulated the London Stock Exchange. This relaxation of rules, known as the Big Bang, spelled the end of old-fashioned trading floors and the beginning of electronic investing.

Still, the sole gateway into markets was through **financial advisers** and **stockbrokers**. Their services were only available face to face in family offices or over the phone. Buying investments or getting advice from these middlemen (and they were usually men) was time consuming and expensive. Their knowledge of the markets was a fiercely guarded secret.

But changes were already afoot. A big moment was the **privatisation** of British Telecom (BT), which was the first time the government sold a state-owned utility to private investors. This occurred through **flotation** – i.e. when a company registers (or **lists**) on the stock market so people can own shares in it.

A huge marketing campaign was targeted at ordinary people to encourage them to buy. It worked: more than three million shares went on sale at an affordable price of 130p and by the time the offer closed, they were more than three times oversubscribed.

Many other companies and utilities followed suit, including British Gas with its famous TV campaign imploring folks to "tell Sid" about the upcoming share sale. This catapulted business from the bowels of the *Financial Times* into the mainstream media.

The long-term performance of these new shares was, well, mixed (soz, Sid), but it was the start of stock market investing as we know it today.

Let's get digital

AS THE 1990S and 2000s wore on, financial companies started upgrading their back-office technology and digitalising more of their services.

The commercialisation of the internet in the mid-1990s also sparked the creation of **platforms** (or **fund supermarkets/shops**) where Sid could now trade online.

These platforms were set up by **execution-only stockbrokers**, also known as **discount brokers**, whose name indicates they only execute orders placed by customers through their websites and don't give any financial advice. This paved the way for DIY – do it yourself – investing.

Platforms quickly became popular because they also started selling **mutual funds** (or **unit trusts**), which pool people's money in a portfolio of different investments chosen by a fund manager. This is known as **active investing**.

Pre-internet, you could only buy these funds directly from the **investment houses** operating them by sending off a form printed in the newspaper (old school!). Now, you can buy them cheaply and easily from online fund supermarkets.

Soon, a challenger came from across the pond in the form of **tracker funds**, invented by investment firm Vanguard, which simply buy or 'track' all the shares in an index (i.e. a basket of assets) and require much less input from a manager. This approach is described as **passive investing**.

All this coincided with the rise of many **dot-com** companies with catchy names and a promise to get big fast. Web-based firms got early funding through **venture capital**, where institutions and professional investors cough up cash for a slice of a start-up's profits once it becomes successful. But many first-time investors also piled in, thanks to the first internet stockbrokers.

This was a peculiar time when media-hungry entrepreneurs headed up companies that made zero profit but were valued spectacularly and saw their share prices go through the roof.

Some businesses from this heady era have gone on to change the world, like Amazon. But most didn't. This period is called the **dot-com bubble** because most of the businesses were way overvalued and the bubble burst, with shares quickly collapsing by $5 trillion.[71] Half of all internet companies founded in 1996 went bust by 2004.[72]

I wanted to know what the early days of internet investing were like. I asked someone who was there – Simon Bain, former business editor at the *Herald* newspaper (who also happens to be my dad!). He said:

> I vividly remember buying my first shares, in early 2001. All I had to do was open an account with Direct Sharedeal, one of the new online brokers, and with a few clicks I had become an investor.

> I bought BT, convinced it was cheap at the time (it wasn't). It wasn't a great time to be a beginner, as the dot-com bubble was about to burst. But I felt a great sense of financial empowerment in being able to get the same opportunities that in the past had only been open to rich folk with a stockbroker.

Investing at the peak of a bubble? Like I would ever do such a thing! (See my investing diary in the last chapter.)

The point is that the internet unlocked far more investing opportunities for the public. But even by this point, investing wasn't mass market or youth-friendly. It would take another decade for internet banking to kick off, followed by the smartphone finance revolution.

Smart money

THE 2010S USHERED in a whole new generation of financial start-ups thanks to big improvements in technology. They embraced cloud and serverless computing to cut overhead costs, pushing the investing revolution even further beyond those with existing wealth and insider knowledge. This period really gave birth to the concept of **fintech** – a portmanteau of fin-ancial and tech-nology.

First up, there were **robo-advisers** (or **digital wealth managers**). Traditional wealth managers provide investment advice and management to the well-off – usually with at least six figures to invest. And those who can afford it pay high fees for the privilege.

Nutmeg launched in 2012 to offer an affordable alternative: ready-made investment **portfolios** – i.e. a collection of carefully chosen investments – but costing only 0.6% of the investments' value per year.

How is this possible? Firstly, **algorithms**. These gather relevant information from prospective investors (usually through a questionnaire) to match them to the right portfolio, making the whole process more efficient. Secondly, robo-advisers use a cheaper kind of investment known as **ETFs**, a more modern spin on passive investing, both of which we'll deal with in due course.

As people began to manage their lives through their phones, the online brokers started to move with the times. Hargreaves Lansdown, the biggest player in that market, launched its app in 2011. But a new business model was just around the corner.

Robinhood, which launched in the US in 2014, scrapped the **commission** that stockbrokers and wealth managers traditionally charged on trading, kickstarting a craze for **free trading** apps, which FreeTrade has continued in the UK.

This led to an additional market known as **social trading**, which eToro spearheaded. It offers the chance to copy certain 'star' trader portfolios and participate in league tables.

By 2015, there were 200 robo-advisers in the US, and one took things a step further. Stash allowed you to buy fractions of shares to lower the cost of investing even more. Cue the rise of **fractional trading** (or **fractional shares**), where investors could now buy small slices of hot but expensive shares like Apple for just a few dollars or pounds.

We also saw that same year the launch of **micro-investing** (or **spare change** investing) through a UK app called Moneybox, which rounds up your spending and sweeps the spare change into one of three attractive portfolios. By now, investing had reached peak millennial: you could buy shares every time you bought avo brunch! Woo-hoo!

Vanguard also stepped up a gear in 2017 when it launched its UK platform, offering investors the chance to directly buy its cut-price tracker funds and ETFs, before launching the cheapest-ever personal pension in 2020.

And before any of this second digital wave happened, there was the mysterious invention of an entirely new digital-only currency in 2009: Bitcoin. I will explain the essentials of **cryptocurrency** in chapter 17, as this (and the **blockchain** technology behind it) has had major ramifications for internet finance.

Investing anywhere, anytime

OUR FINANCIAL LIVES have changed beyond recognition. Now you can buy almost any kind of investment using your phone while on the treadmill, in bed or at your second cousin's wedding (none of which is advisable, BTW).

And to think – my dad, when he was my age, could only buy shares in a handful of British companies *by post*. And when he started investing in the early 2000s, he had to fire up his gigantic desk-bound PC and wait for the internet to dial up before placing an order. Lol.

Digital investing is here to stay. But it's a diverse and complex market, so you need to carefully weigh up the different options so you can make the right choice. And that choice will definitely be influenced by how you view the biggest dividing line in investing, with both sides locked in a fierce battle for your money.

Yep, it's the active versus passive smackdown. Have no idea what I'm talking about? Let me set the scene so you understand the big fight better…

CHAPTER 12

Active or passive?

THE ACTIVE VERSUS passive debate has raged in the world of finance for donkey's years, and it doesn't come with easy answers. But you've got to be informed about this stuff before you jump into investing because it will play a major part in your decision about what you invest in and which services to use.

As we saw in the last chapter, lots of things have changed in finance over the past few decades. One thing that's remained constant is the dominant role of fund platforms in the UK. As of August 2020, Hargreaves Lansdown has over a million customers with a near 50% share of the entire investment platform market.

Another reason for the success of platforms, particularly HL, has been their enthusiastic promotion of Britain's powerful mutual fund industry, which now manages more than a TRILLION pounds of our money in the UK.

Active funds have often been put forward as a good way for ordinary investors to access the stock market if they don't want the responsibility of picking their own shares. But funds – or rather, the people managing them – can be fallible, and it's not always in the industry's interests to point out that there may be alternatives that cost less and perform better. Before we get into that, let's look at how funds work.

Welcome to the house of funds

AN **INVESTMENT FUND** or **mutual fund** is a collective pool of money – not just your cash but loads of other people's too. This money is managed as a giant mass and put into assets. They are also known as **open-ended funds** because they can issue an unlimited number of shares. There is another type of active fund called an **investment trust**, which is a **closed-ended** investment because it is set up as a company that can issue only a limited number of shares. We'll explore how trusts work in chapter 18.

Funds are overseen by humans to make sure things don't go wrong, but the degree to which they are managed by humans varies. An **active fund** is headed up by a fund manager (or two), usually with a team of analysts. They make active investing decisions on your behalf, creating a portfolio of assets they have selected, with the aim of delivering the best return possible.

Active funds always have a goal or **mandate**. It might be to invest in a specific market, like technology, a country or region (e.g. China or Europe), or companies of a certain size, from big ones to small ones and lots in between. They'll also have different approaches to investing, like 'value' or 'growth', which we'll get into in chapter 20.

There are sound reasons why active funds have been popular. They allow you to outsource the minutiae of investing to other people – the financial equivalent of going to a top restaurant and getting the chef to cook you a meal rather than having to find all the ingredients, use exactly the right quantities and time the prep perfectly yourself.

Investing in a selection of funds can also be a neat way to ensure you're not putting all your eggs in one basket – i.e. that you are **diversifying** your investments, another majorly important principle in investing.

Plus, you might find picking shares yourself both hard AND scary. When you invest in active funds, a professional fund manager is doing the work for you.

But Little Miss Cynic here wonders if another reason why funds have ruled the roost is because they can be pretty lucrative for the people pushing them.

Active promotion

IT'S FAIR TO say there are quite a few parties that benefit from the promotion of active funds. For starters, there are platforms that tend to steer people towards active funds by predominantly recommending them in 'best buy' lists. Research by Boring Money suggests that a quarter of investors rely on these lists, while a further 45% use them as a "secondary sense check".[73]

While platforms insist their lists are never guided by commercial factors, it's worth noting the bigger platforms earn commission from selling mutual funds, and active funds in particular give them more scope for a juicy fee.

Active funds also get a lot of airtime in the financial media, but you probably don't realise that fund houses have big budgets to take journalists out to the pub, theatre, sporting fixtures and dinner at top restaurants. Being a journalist myself, I know the effort the media makes to be independent. But it's difficult when so much material needed to adequately cover the world of investing (like market analysis) is so helpfully supplied by platforms and the fund industry.

Last but not least, active managers themselves earn an **annual management charge** (AMC) of between 0.75% and 1.25% of the value of funds under management, and sometimes an additional performance fee.

In the long term, as a percentage on millions or even billions of pounds, boy those charges stack up. Active fund managers also receive big salaries and/or bonuses. Those overseeing funds worth billions of pounds sometimes have an annual income of seven figures.

In other words, a lot of people are making a lot of money and getting to enjoy the finer things in life thanks to the active fund model. And this really sticks in the craw when you consider evidence that many – perhaps most – active fund managers aren't producing better long-term returns than a computer, despite costing more.

Track to basics

I MENTIONED TRACKER or index funds in the last chapter – they simply 'track' the assets in an index. Just to remind you, an index is a measure that's used to monitor the performance of certain assets in a standard, consistent way. For example, the FTSE 100 is an index of the 100 biggest companies in the UK.

When you invest in a tracker fund, the performance of the investment will very closely match the performance of the index that the fund is set up to track. Therefore, a FTSE 100 tracker fund will provide investors in the fund with the performance of the FTSE 100.

Tracker funds just need a reliable bot that will accurately track the performance of the index, plus some humans to make sure the fund rebalances and reflects any significant changes in the assets it tracks.

Tracker funds don't have expensive human fund managers and teams of analysts to pay, so this makes them a lot cheaper than active funds, with fees usually ranging between 0.1% and 0.85%. This doesn't sound that different from the AMCs charged by fund managers, but over time, on lots of cash, trust me, it is.

There's pretty much one man who is singlehandedly responsible for the tracker concept – the late John C. (or 'Jack') Bogle. He set up the Vanguard Group in 1975 and went on to launch the First Index Investment Trust in 1976. His most famous quote is: "Don't look for the needle in the haystack – just buy the haystack!"

By this, he meant that it's impossible to find the few star investments, i.e. the proverbial needles, in an index. You stand a much greater chance of capturing their success if you buy the whole index cheaply.

When Jack Bogle died in 2019, *Forbes* magazine tweeted that he left behind a "collection of devoted acolytes and millions of investors whose retirements will be fatter because Bogle spread his gospel."[74]

UK investment market: passive is taking an increasing share

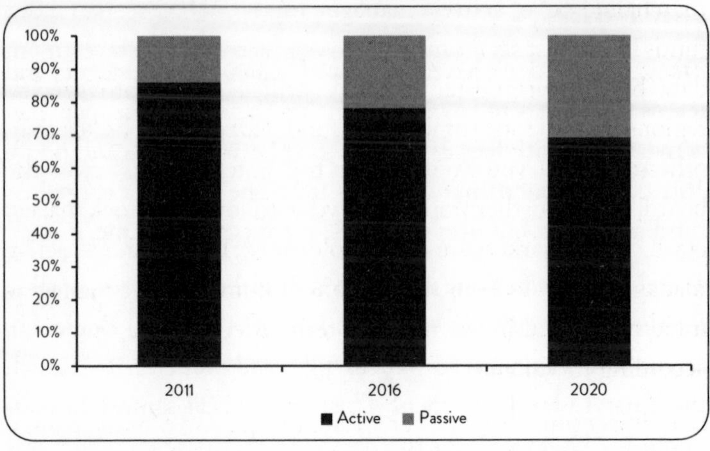

Source: Statista

So, do tracker funds *really* make your funds fatter? Quite possibly. An independent study by Cass Business School in 2014 concluded that between 1998 and 2008, a typical investor would have been 1.44% a year better off by switching from their active fund to a low-cost passive UK equity tracker. It claimed that only 1% of active managers generated superior performance – and this could easily be swallowed up in the higher fees you pay for active managers.[75]

Passive aggressive

A BIG CLAIM made on behalf of active funds is that when stock markets tumble, so do tracker funds – because they blindly match what happens in the index they are tracking. By contrast, human managers can spot opportunities to protect investors' money when stock markets fall and capitalise on any rebounds when the markets rise again. But is that really true?

When stock markets crashed due to coronavirus in 2020, fewer than half (43%) of actively managed funds did better than index funds in the first six months of the year, according to investment data boffs Morningstar.[76] If you drilled down into specific regions and sectors, some active funds fared much better than others; but still, you would expect top-notch returns across the board, right? Furthermore, in the years following a stock market crash (when markets are in the doldrums), history shows active managers may do even worse: 60% of human active managers underperformed in the medium term after the dot-com crash, according to Vanguard.[77]

Let's inject some balance here. You can slice and dice the data to present a more nuanced picture: there have been and continue to be incredibly successful active fund managers. For instance, Fundsmith Equity, managed by Terry Smith, produced an astounding 420% return in the ten years after its launch in 2010 – more than double that of the MSCI World Index, against which it is typically measured. Though who knows if that stellar track record will continue?

Also, there are fears that passively investing in a market that is increasingly dominated by huge tech companies (like Apple, Microsoft and Amazon) will lead to massive losses in tracker funds if any of these companies should crash and burn.[78]

Still, it's hard to overstate just how influential the active vs passive ruckus has been in the investment world. It divides investors into two camps – one that prefers to actively invest through funds, investment trusts or simply picking out assets, and the other that prefers to passively invest in index funds and a more modern offshoot of passive investing that has REALLY come to the fore in recent years: ETFs.

ETF phone home

EXCHANGE-TRADED FUNDS (COMMONLY known as **ETFs**) also aim to shadow promising parts of the stock market – but they are structured in a different way from index funds.

Here, the fund house buys the underlying assets, designs a fund – the ETF – to track them and then sells shares in the fund for you to buy. You should then get the spoils of the underlying assets doing well thanks to the value of your share rising. Equally, your share in the ETF would fall if the underlying assets lose value.

Other funds are only traded once a day, so while you can buy or sell them at any time, the trade doesn't happen straightaway but at the next 'trade point' (usually the end of the day). By contrast, an ETF can be bought and sold like a share on the stock market at any time.

ETFs have exploded in the past decade because they are such a simple way to package index investing for your average Joe and Joanne. They've become a lot more sophisticated too, often programmed to adopt the same strategy that a human would take to maximise returns and reduce risk.

All this helps to explain why ETFs now dominate the passive school of investing and help to power those cheaper robo-advisers I mentioned in chapter 11. But ETFs are also now available to buy through fund supermarkets, most freetrading apps and Vanguard's own investing platform. It's the ETF, perhaps above anything else, that poses the biggest existential threat to active fund managers.

Breaking the monopoly

PERHAPS YOU ARE still fund-curious, open to the (valid) idea that there are some active managers out there who could do better than either you OR a bot. If that's the case, you don't want to rule out learning more about established platforms and the huge universe of funds they offer.

Nonetheless, I am glad to see lower-cost alternatives to the traditional platforms AND the active funds they push. The symbiotic relationship between these two industries has been too cosy for too long.

What's more, ETFs may well be the game changer that gets a whole new generation investing for the first time, and there's a reason that younger investors – particularly those wanting to retire early – are fanatical about them (see my bonus chapter in part 1).

So, now we understand the broader investing context, there are some more specific things you'll need to think through. What kind of investor do you want to be? How much time and effort are you willing to put in? How much risk do you want to take?

All those questions might make you go, "OMG, I have NO idea." If so, there's one type of investment app that might provide some answers. Ride on, robos!

CHAPTER 13

How robo-advisers work

BY NOW, YOU may start to get a sense of how hands-on an investor you want to be. You may be tantalised by all the opportunities out there and itching to learn more about them. But some people have their limits.

Robo-advice, or digital wealth management, may be right for you if you decide at the end of this book that you want to outsource pretty much everything to one app. Even if you already suspect that's the case, I recommend you keep reading beyond this chapter. You will get so much more out of your investing experience if you really grasp all the concepts involved.

But still, many young people simply want to be guided towards a sensible investing portfolio – maybe one that's socially responsible too – so that they can get on with their lives.

You may be one of them. So, what are your next steps?

The price of advice

THE OBVIOUS ANSWER would be to consult an independent financial adviser (IFA). They find out why you want to invest, ask how much risk you are comfortable with, check out your personal circumstances and put you into some suitable investments.

You may be thinking: "Great, where do I sign up?"

Well, I hate to break it to ya, but a study by Schroders found that in 2017, half of all IFAs turned away clients with less than £50,000 to invest.

That may help to explain why only 6% of 18–34-year-olds took financial advice in 2017. Based on the empirical and anecdotal evidence I have seen, the figures haven't improved much in more recent years.

Regulations introduced in 2013 outlawed 'free advice' which was actually funded by disguised commissions paid to the adviser. In one way, this was a positive move, helping to clean up an industry that had been historically rife with mis-selling. Dodgier advisers would push funds which – unbeknownst to the client – were paying the highest commissions.

This rule change had the unintended but entirely predictable consequence that (most) IFAs started taking their fees from a percentage cut of assets under management, so that only richer clients were worth their while. In any event, the 'young, gifted and broke' have never been meat and drink for the UK's £4.5bn financial advice industry: their speciality is complex stuff like high-value estate planning and pensions.

Fortunately, enlightened advisers out there are starting to take an interest in young investors: let's hope they can turn the tide. In the meantime, let's look at a more affordable alternative.

IFAs doing it for the kids

Neon Financial Planning, based in Nottingham, has a banging website showcasing a range of fixed-fee services, including a free financial health check, financial coaching at £100 for half an hour, access to a Money Info app at £40 a month, and a full financial review at £750. Note that these services are all generic 'guidance', so you're not going to get personal investment recommendations.

The machines take over

IN CHAPTER 11, I introduced robo-advisers as cheaper, digital versions of financial advisers and wealth managers. They'll sell you a portfolio like a craft project on vintage *Blue Peter* – "here's one we made earlier" – through an app that should diagnose your investing needs. So (in theory), you can get over the fact you can't even get through the door of Poshington & Sons.

FYI, most of the robo-adviser community *hate* the term 'robo-adviser' and often use 'digital weath manager' or other descriptions. But the robo tag has firmly stuck, so I'm using it for the sake of recognition.

The main guys to look out for are:*

- Nutmeg
- Wealthify
- Moneyfarm

* This is the most comprehensive list possible at time of writing, excluding robo-advisers that require large minimum investments or players I deemed too small for inclusion.

- WealthSimple
- True Potential
- Wealth Horizon
- Dozens
- Moneybox
- Tickr
- Plum
- IG Smart
- OpenMoney.

Let's look at robos' main features:

1. **They're fairly simple to use.** You can probably open a portfolio with most of these guys in the time it would take to water the plants or (in my case) buy some new plants to replace the last ones that you killed.
2. **They take on small sums.** There is often no minimum investment amount required and most allow affordable starting sums.
3. **They generally use ETFs.** As mentioned in chapter 12, ETFs help to push down your investing costs. But note that Wealthify uses active funds for smaller portfolios, while Moneybox opts for tracker funds.
4. **They try to nail down your risk appetite to suggest the best portfolio for you.** You might go through a questionnaire or simply be asked to assess yo'self. Many will put you between a 1 and a 5 on the risk spectrum, with 1 being Cautious and 5 being Adventurous or Aggressive. The middle, 3, is usually Balanced.

5. **Some ask what your life goals are and how long you'll be investing for.** That way, you can be funnelled into not only the right investments but the right wrapper, like a LISA, stocks and shares ISA or pension.

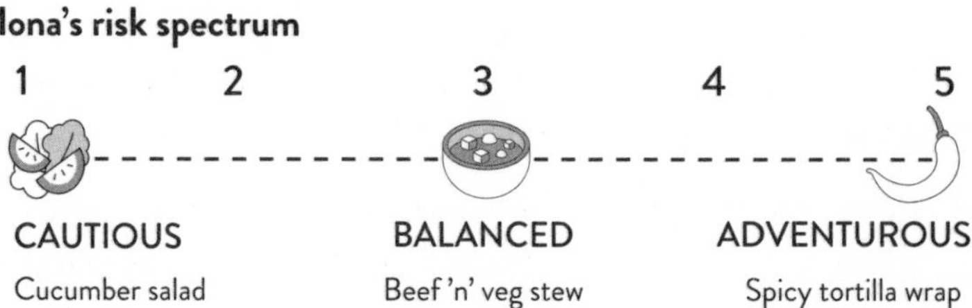

Moneybox and the theory behind micro-investing

When **Moneybox** launched in 2016, it offered users the chance to round up spare change from their daily spending into a stocks and shares ISA. It uses nudge theory, the same concept behind auto enrolment in pensions, to coax people into investing.

It works by linking your debit or credit card to Moneybox. When you use your card – say, to buy a £2.50 coffee – Moneybox debits £3, rerouting the extra 50p into one of its investment accounts. Moneybox also allows you to invest higher sums when the mood takes you.

It sounds ingenious and Moneybox is great for beginner investors who have shaky income or just want to just dip their toes in the markets. But micro-investing won't get you far, particularly if you have ambitious investment goals It's really just a clever trick to ease you into robo-advice. Only a minority of Moneybox users stick with micro-investing, with most switching to a larger and regular direct debit within months.

Robo a gogo

HERE IS WHAT I rate about robos:

✓ They're genuinely pulling in a new crowd. Around four in ten of Nutmeg's 60,000 customers (at time of writing) have never invested before and 35% are women (the market average for female investors is 26%).

✓ Robos are trying to be responsible towards inexperienced investors – for example, Wealthify and OpenMoney will tell you not to invest if they don't think you're a suitable candidate.

✓ Most hold your hand through what could be a difficult process. Working out your investing timeframe and attitude to risk is central to investing and it's all too easy to skip that when you're picking out shares or funds.

✓ Some allow you to make more proactive investing choices, but in a safe(ish) space. Of course, investing is never risk free, but if you become more informed and want to tap into certain sectors or markets for promising growth, then Plum offers portfolios like 'Best of British' and 'American Dream' (see box opposite).

✓ Some provide actively or fully managed portfolios, but still based on ETFs. So, backroom teams can monitor your portfolio closely and make changes to try and improve its prospects at a lower cost than a traditional active investment fund. And the research does seem to indicate that – so far – robos perform better than your average British human stock picker.[79]

✓ They usually describe their portfolios in a way that anyone can understand. No bollocks about 'alpha returns'. Many offer socially responsible portfolios that you'd struggle to put together yourself on a free-trading app or a fund platform.

Indeed, Tickr offers nothing but socially responsible options – peace out, guys.

✓ The customer service is generally good, with help available by phone, email and live chat.

✓ Most robos have a wealth of educational material on investing, usually found on the 'Blog' sections of their websites (but not always accessible through their apps). Robos specialise in practical guides to personal finance and investments, often presented as online courses and academies, but do offer some topical analysis on stock markets.

✓ They're super-attractive, with cool features like risk sliders. Anything that makes investing feel pleasurable and cutting edge is not to be sniffed at!

Plum – the first investment chatbot

Money chatbots (or AI assistants) are one of the latest types of fintech shaking up the banking market. They link up to your bank account, tell you how much money you have, work out how much and when you save, and prompt you to do it – all through matey messages and fun GIFs. But Plum goes beyond its competitors by offering an investment option, making it the first robo-adviser cum chatbot.

It has the expected three risk-based funds for beginners and clearly tells you these are actually ETFs run by Vanguard, with 20%, 60% or 80% levels of equities and the remainder in bonds. But it also has another six themed funds, inviting investors to "own a piece of Google and Apple, ride the wave of emerging markets like China and Brazil, or back socially responsible companies".

While robo-advisers pick out the supposedly more ethical or best-practice companies across the whole investing world,

Plum's other choices involve making more of an investment call. Do you go for the biggest companies in the US, or the UK, or Europe? Or dare you "invest in the growth of new giants in Asia and Africa" – known in fund-speak as **emerging markets** investing? Or should you follow the lure of Apple, Microsoft, and the other tech giants?

Plum tells you what the funds would have generated if they had been running from 2015 to 2020, but remember that this is hypothetical – Plum only launched in 2017 – and we know by now that the past is no precise guide to the future. The Tech Giants fund would have returned an average 25% a year, with its other five options showing returns of between 3% (Best of British) and 15% (American Dream).

Plum is being more imaginative than its competitors by offering what's usually called **thematic investing** – that is, investing in specific markets or sectors. But a little knowledge can be a dangerous thing. You may look at tech's phenomenal returns and decide that looks like a better bet than beleaguered old Blighty, for instance. But you would be basing that decision on what's happened, not what's to come.

You need to make a judgement call as to whether yesterday's winners will continue to streak ahead or, if over the next five years, the out-of-favour UK market will bounce back from a low base. It's a big step up from normal robo considerations and all these funds are classed at risk levels of 5 or 6 (out of 7), so they're not for the fainthearted.

Robo no-no

NOW, HERE ARE some of things about robos I'm not so keen on:

- ✗ Robos tend to emphasise their platform fee, which makes them *look* cheap compared to other options, but you also have to add on the fund fee and perhaps a flat monthly charge. Some websites make these charges easier to unpick than others! And some portfolios cost more than others. For instance, Nutmeg has a 0.45% platform fee and an average 0.17% cost for its funds, making the average total 0.62%. But the 'managed' or socially responsible fund options are more expensive at 0.94% and 1.07%. Be aware that when you see fees quoted online, they tend to be based on the middle-risk option.
- ✗ The average fund fee for robos is 0.26%, which sounds cheap, especially when compared to non-robo platforms offering their own in-house funds (0.65%). But taken all together, the average monthly cost of investing £100 a month in robos is £7.30, compared to £6.28 with the non-robos if you exclude one high charger (Barclays). And if you plump for DIY investing, you can pay as little as £2 a month with some platforms and £1 with Vanguard if you're happy to use its funds.[80] All this means that some robos, offering certain portfolios, can work out just as expensive – if not more – than investing through a platform, while none come as cheaply as investing in ETFs, for instance through Vanguard's own platform.[81] So, if your robo underperforms, you'll have the worst of all worlds: none of the raw bargain benefits of ETF investing and none of the potential outperformance offered by good active fund managers.

✗ Being able to open a portfolio with £1? Big deal. It's not a great selling point for anyone serious about getting started.

✗ It's too early to say whether robos are performing well, compared to other investing options. Wealthsimple's portfolios performed better than those at Nutmeg, Wealthify and Moneyfarm in 2019, according to one analysis.[82] But another suggested that in the early 2020 coronavirus market wipeout, only one robo-adviser conserved investors' money better than Vanguard's comparable LifeStrategy fund in low-risk portfolios – that was OpenMoney.[83] In medium-risk portfolios, the robo-adviser that dropped the least was IG Smart. Even that isn't a complete picture, as Nutmeg declined to offer data. Still, according to its own website, *all* Nutmeg's portfolios lagged Vanguard's equivalents in the 12 months up to June 2020. We should know by now *not* to assess investments' long-term prospects based on just one year. And TBF, robo-advisers haven't been around that long, so maybe it's only right to wait a few more years before making any further judgements.

✗ Offering 'cautious' investments, while well-intentioned, could end up doing more harm than good. Younger investors might play safer than they really should. Once you hit that investment starting grid, in many cases you're better off in the faster lane, so long as you know you won't need that money for at least five years.

✗ Risk ratings may be unreliable. The Financial Conduct Authority (FCA) has found various problems with the way some companies did their risk profiling of investors, known officially as the **suitability assessment**.[84] Robos lean heavily on questionnaires, decision trees and algorithms; but if the profiling is not subtle enough and you are put in the wrong box, you could end up taking too much risk and losing money, or too little risk and missing your investment goals.

✗ Despite their name, many robo-advisers don't actually offer financial advice. (Duh duh DUHHHHH!) Bet you didn't see that twist coming...

In fact, it's not fair to compare robo-advisers to financial advisers, as they don't offer the same service. Many robo-advisers don't have permission (yet) to offer regulated financial advice, which means they can't offer personal recommendations on what to do (or not do) with your money. Instead, they stick to 'guidance' – narrowing down the options and leaving you to decide your own appetite for risk – or simplified advice, where you provide detailed info that's processed by an algorithm that lands you in the most suitable risk zone. The latter's only responsibility under financial regulation is to make sure the risk zone matches your declared circumstances.

By contrast, the fully regulated financial adviser must take a holistic view of your finances, then recommend specific products and funds. They are legally responsible for making sure this entire advice is suitable. So, you can complain to the Financial Ombudsman Service or the Financial Services Compensation Scheme if you received inappropriate advice – say, you were advised to put money into a needlessly high-risk investment, perhaps unregulated or offshore – from a regulated financial adviser and lost money as a result.

Besides, what happens if there's a market crash and you're tempted to cash in your whole portfolio? Fully regulated advisers can save you from making this kind of dumb-ass decision.

Fortunately, the market is evolving in the right direction, with firms starting to offer a combination of both generic guidance AND full advice. Nutmeg now offers bespoke advice for £350, promising personal interaction over the phone or face to face. OpenMoney offers full financial advice alongside its robo platform and money management app, making it one of the most complete financial services I've come across. Wealthsimple and Moneyfarm also provide full investment advice and have human advisers on hand.

Dozens – the one-stop shop for your finances?

There is a newish kid on the block called Dozens. It combines a current account, saving/budgeting tools, including micro saving, AND an investment provider, all in one app. It even pays cash prizes to people who manage their finances well (wonders never cease!). It has a limited access savings bond paying 5%, which it says is funded by "the revenues earned from our other products".[85]

Like Plum, it invites you to think a bit about what you want to invest in. Alongside the expected ESG option, there are options to invest in emerging markets, "or big trends like robotics and cyber security". Each of these are represented by a single fund, an ETF or an **ETC (Exchange Traded Commodity)**. It only charges its 0.5% fee when your investments are in the black and promises "prompts" to keep your portfolio on track. But like so many robo-advisers, it doesn't offer fully regulated financial advice.

Robo flop?

IT'S TEMPTING TO buy into the narrative that robo-advisers will make IFAs and traditional investment platforms redundant, particularly among young investors. But in fact, robo-advisers have had a very rocky ride.

Take the British digital wealth manager, Moola, which was wound up in 2020 with a turnover of just £3,768. Then there's Click & Invest, shut by its South African parent company Investec in 2019; while Swiss bank UBS shut its baby, SmartWealth, the previous year, admitting its near-term potential was "limited". Indeed, at time of writing, UK-based Nutmeg is yet to make a profit despite (or maybe because of) advertising campaigns designed to lure new investors.

Still, robo-advisers aren't going away. I think the market is only set to grow – albeit with fewer companies in a survival of the fittest.[86] We'll also likely see more firms offering backup financial advice in the future, as many already do in the US, making them much more comprehensive (and safer).

Robo-advisers have certainly done their bit to democratise investment. They can be a pathway into investing for beginners with small sums but big dreams. They help you think about risk and your goals before responsibly narrowing down the vast investment universe in a way many newbies find comforting.

But no app can eliminate the risks of investing entirely and robos come with their own hazards, from giving you the wrong steer on risk, overcharging you for investments you can get more cheaply elsewhere, or being unable to stop you making terrible decisions.

Robos are no substitute for a real investment education. The truth is that you can't just outsource all the decisions to an algorithm and forgeddaboutit. You've still got to understand what it takes to be an efficient, level-headed investor today.

Nonetheless, if you read the rest of this book and decide DIY investing isn't for you, here's a table I put together to help you compare the main robos out there. This data was correct at the time of writing, but things can change and so you should double check yourself for the latest figures.

Note that the table excludes the premature and relatively incomplete measures of the robos' performance so far.

It's worth having a look at each of the robos' websites to get a feel for which one would be best for you.

Robo	Minimum investment	Pricing[1]	Investment	Risk spectrum	Socially responsible option?	Financial advice?
Nutmeg*	£500	0.62%[2]	ETFs	5–10 portfolios	Yes	Yes
Wealthify	£1	0.82%	ETFs	5 portfolios	Yes	No
Moneyfarm	£1500	0.95%[3]	ETFs	7 portfolios	No	Yes
Wealth Simple	£1	0.9%[4]	ETFs	9 portfolios	Yes	Yes
Tickr	£5	0.67% + £1 a month[5]	ETFs	4 themes, 3 risk levels	All options are socially responsible	No
True Potential Investor	£50	1.16%	Funds	10 portfolios	No	No[6]
Wealth Horizon	£1000	0.89%[7]	Funds	5 levels	No	Yes
Dozens	£1000	1.07%[8]	ETFs	5 levels	Yes	No
Moneybox*	£1	0.66% + £1 a month[9]	Tracker funds	3 levels	Yes	No
Plum	£1	0.53% + £1 a month	ETFs	3 levels	Yes	No
IG Smart	£500	0.72%[10]	ETFs	5 levels	No	No
OpenMoney	£1	0.51%	ETFs	3 levels	No	Yes

Notes on table

* Offers Lifetime ISA

1. Please note all pricing is based on platform/ISA charge + mid-risk fund charge.
2. Fixed allocation portfolio. 'Managed' 0.94%, socially responsible 1.07%.
3. 0.95% up to £10k, 0.8% on £10–50k then sliding scale.
4. Over £100k cost 0.7%.
5. 0% fee on balances below £3k.
6. True Potential Wealth Management offers financial advice.
7. £25 initial charge.
8. No platform fee if fund is showing a loss.
9. First three months free.
10. Over £50k cost 0.47%.

CHAPTER 14

Do-it-yourself investing: the deal with platforms

WE'RE MOVING INTO higher-stakes territory now as we tackle **DIY investing**.

If using a robo (or real) adviser is like buying all your furniture from the showroom and paying for it to be delivered, DIY investing is like getting all the materials (or maybe a flatpack from IKEA) and building your living space from scratch.

That might sound daunting. But as with home interiors, DIY investing could get you a more tailormade result at much lower cost – but only if it's carefully done. Otherwise, prepare to make some expensive mistakes, and much worse ones than using the wrong screw.

Should you decide to go DIY, a key question will be which platform or trading site to use. On the one hand, there are traditional platforms. These provide an unrivalled choice of investments and tax-efficient wrappers, often stuffed with expert analysis to help you make wiser decisions. In other words, they can be a strong option for beginner investors.

On the other hand, there are alternatives like Vanguard and Freetrade, both undercutting the traditional players with cheaper models but a more limited range of investments. We'll deal with those in due course but first, let's cover the remaining issues we haven't yet discussed in relation to platforms.

Platforms: pros and problems

MOST PLATFORMS HAVE been established by specialised players like Hargreaves Lansdown, Interactive Investor and AJ Bell Youinvest, which are the big three. Banks have also got in on the act, like Halifax with its iWeb and Halifax Share Dealing platforms.

Here are some of the others:

- Interactive Investor (branded ii)
- Barclays Smart
- BestInvest
- HSBC
- Fidelity
- Aviva
- Charles Stanley Direct
- Cavendish
- Close Brothers
- Santander
- Willis Owen.

Here are the main features of platforms:

1. They offer nearly all mainstream investments, with a wide choice of active and tracker funds, investment trusts, ETFs, individual shares and bonds.
2. They provide most of the tax-efficient wrappers that younger investors will be considering, such as stocks and shares ISAs and personal pensions.

3. When you sign up for a platform, there will be an annual charge or account fee, typically around 0.5%. There might be a combination of a fixed monthly fee plus trading costs, or just the trading cost for making an investment. On top of that are the charges on your actual investment fund, or your 'strategy'. These range from under 0.05% for a low-cost ETF to 1.5% or higher for a specialist active fund. If you buy investment trusts, ETFs or individual shares, there will be transaction costs based on the **spread** (i.e difference in price) between buying and selling, typically adding under 0.1% to the bill.
4. Many have recommended fund lists and in-house portfolios, built around different risk profiles. Unlike robo-advisers, these portfolios aren't created with ETFs, but with a range of assets or active/passive funds. Hargreaves Lansdown, for example, runs its own **multi-manager** funds, which are portfolios comprising of lots of other funds.
5. Most have apps and mobile functionality, but they tend to have desktop-first websites.

Are my investments safe if my investing site goes bust?

A platform, robo-adviser or trading app must hold your investments separate from its business, so if it goes bust your investments are ring-fenced. If fraud has taken place and the company can't afford to reimburse you, then the Financial Services Compensation Scheme would step in, but this only protects you up to £85,000 per firm.

Here are some of the things I like about traditional platforms:

✓ They let you get in the driving seat.[87] Whether you plump for active funds, investment trusts, ETFs, individual shares or off-the-shelf portfolios, platforms have got you (mostly) covered. They don't assume they know best – they let you decide what to do with your money and they don't close off options in a way that might become frustrating as time goes on.

✓ On some platforms, you can reduce trading costs on shares, investment trusts and ETFs by setting up regular monthly investing. This is known as **drip-feeding**, i.e. investing regularly in markets, and is a neat strategy all beginner investors should consider. It means you are smoothing out the price you are paying for a particular share over time, which may be frustrating when prices are rising, but reassuring when they are falling. It's also cheaper: AJ Bell and Hargreaves both charge £1.50 per stock for automatic investing on the same day each month – compared with up to £9.95 and £11.95 respectively for instant trading.

✓ They provide waaayyyy more info than robo-advisers about the investments themselves, though there are some limits: active managers only tell you the top ten holdings they have in any fund.

✓ Many platforms come with an absolute stack of additional content on investing, written by top financial experts. They often employ teams of former financial journalists and advisers with years of experience to analyse what's happening in the markets. Naturally, their content is more comprehensive, topical and authoritative compared to robo-advisers.

✓ Many investment platforms have really upped their tech game in recent years, with websites and apps that go toe to toe with robo.

✓ At the other extreme, some platforms are basic bitches and *proud of it*, like Halifax iWeb. No app, cartoon owls, sliders or investing academies here, but it's HELLA cheap. Some platforms offer better value than robo-advisers if you know exactly what you want to invest in.

Why costs matter

I know I bang on about costs, but they matter. Think of it this way: every 1% deducted from your fund in costs means you need to make an extra 1% return. So, it's not surprising that charges have been found to be the single most important element in reducing investment returns.

For instance, if you invest £100 a month for ten years with total charges of 1% a year, your pot would be worth £500 more than if you paid fees of 1.85%. After 20 years the difference would be £3,000 and after 40 years it would be £20,000. But remember that 'cheap' does not always equal 'good': you should be looking for a platform that offers the best mix of service and price.

Extra investment returns when fee drops from 1.85% to 1%

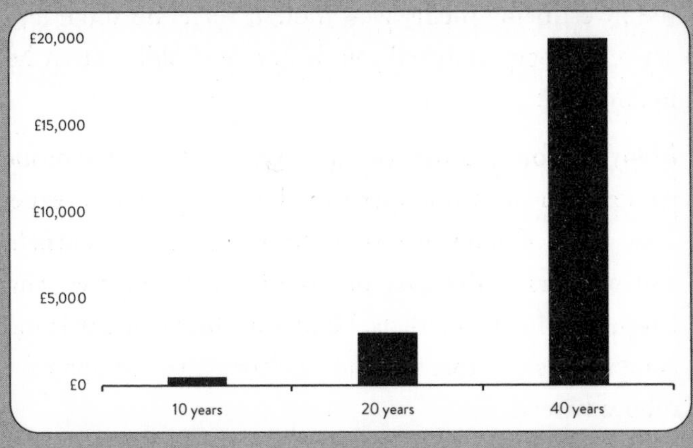

Source: OpenMoney

Here are some things about traditional platforms I'm not so keen on:

✗ Platform costs are even harder to compare than with robo-advisers, and that's saying something. I'm not even going to try and compare all the different platform costs here because it would make your head explode. It depends on what you buy, how much you invest and how often you trade. I have some pointers at the end of this chapter which should help.

✗ Service and functionality are a mixed bag. Some receive mostly positive user reviews online (though you need to make sure these are independently verified). But I've come across many horror stories of glitches, crashes and problems with transfers. Maybe that's because they are doing complex stuff, have been around for a long time and more people use them compared to robo-advisers.

✗ Lots of platforms assume prior knowledge and aren't great for new investors. They use a fair bit of jargon and sometimes overwhelm you with information. And they don't generally offer financial advice.

✗ Some platforms still don't offer apps (not joking), while others are, in all honesty, a bit crap. Many haven't yet integrated key features you would expect from an investment app.

✗ In-house portfolios tend to be more expensive than robo-advisers. This is especially true of multi-manager funds.

Passive platform portfolio: could the three Ps work for you?

As mentioned, platforms do offer pre-packaged portfolios in a similar vein to robo-advisers. However, these differ in some key respects: they don't come with financial advice or even a comprehensive risk questionnaire, and they're generally active portfolios, so they cost more.

But there are a few platforms offering cheaper passive portfolios. AJ Bell has three ETF-dominated portfolios, capped at 0.35%, that go for growth: Cautious, Balanced and Adventurous. Cavendish charges 0.15% for its three Low, Medium and High tracker portfolios, while Willis Owen's Cautious, Moderate and Adventurous Portfolios cost 0.15%, 0.16% and 0.2% respectively.

FYI on DIY

UNLESS YOU CHOOSE a robo-adviser to do it for you, you'll have to decide how to do it yourself. Platforms allow much greater choice over your investments compared to robo-advisers. And compared to free or cheap trading apps, they do have their checks and balances to stop you trading away all your money. One upside of complex fees is that they can deter people from trading too much.

So, a platform could be a sound choice if you want to do it yourself, keep your options open, but be a more restrained trader. Some platforms will offer an excellent deal IF you decide to invest at least partly in active funds. Others, meanwhile, will give you low-cost access to a much bigger universe of shares, ETFs and investment trusts compared to Vanguard or free-trading apps.

You probably haven't made up your mind yet – and that's okay! There's still a lot for you to learn. You can come back to this part – and my quick 'n' dirty guide below – IF you decide a platform's right for you but aren't sure which one would be best.

But in the meantime, there's a whole new frontier of DIY investing that's been enticing young investors to go big or go home, one that focuses on ultra-cheap trading in ETFs, investment trusts, shares and even exotic trends like Bitcoin.

The question is: should YOU buy in too?

My quick 'n' dirty guide to finding good-value platforms

- Cheaper platforms tend to be basic bitch but remember, you can always get your investment insights elsewhere!
- In the beginning, platforms charging low percentage-based fees will probably work out cheaper than those with flat charges.
- Once you build up your investment pot, fixed fees start to become better value. That's because percentage fees really add up on larger investment sums, even if the headline charge gets smaller.
- You should review which platform you're using every few years as your funds build and you get into your stride as an investor – then you can figure out if you could be getting a better deal elsewhere.

- If you want to make one active trade a month, regular automatic investing is cheaper than instant trading.
- You can find the latest free guide to platform pricing at langcatfinancial.co.uk. But don't forget that price isn't everything: service and user experience matter too.

CHAPTER 15

Can digital trading make you rich?

Facebook! Apple! Amazon! Netflix! Google!

LET'S FACE IT – these guys kinda run the world now, don't they? Over the past ten years, a band of American tech pioneers have changed our lives.

The meteoric rise of the so-called FAANGs – see what they did there? – has also been the biggest story in investing. People holding shares in these firms in recent times have cleaned up.

In February 2015, someone who invested $10,000 in the biggest 500 companies in the US would have a portfolio worth $16,190 five years later – a still-excellent return of 62%. But if they had invested purely in the FAANGs, they would have a portfolio worth $39,292 – a staggering return of almost 300% – by February 2020.[88]

Performance of FAANGs versus the S&P 500

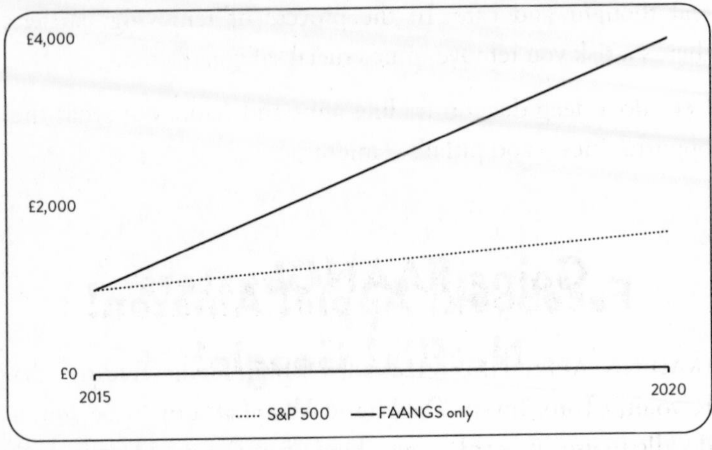

Source: *Investor's Business Daily*

What's behind the astronomical stock market performance of these companies? A major factor is the behaviour of millennials, both as consumers AND investors. The FAANGs are brands we know, rely on, and often love. It seems to make sense to invest in them too.

Plus, when their share prices look like a one-way bet, what's a millennial gonna do when savings rates are a joke and the rest of the stock market looks lame by comparison?

This whole phenomenon underpins the success of a new breed of trading app, specifically designed for da yoof. These highlight millennial-friendly brands, use fleek colour schemes and stars like Alec Baldwin to front their campaigns, focus on 'up-or-down' charts and allow you to start trading in minutes, all at rock-bottom prices. What's not to like?

Well, I'm all for innovation that opens up investing. But when you make investing easy, there's a danger you make it *too* easy.

Investing is still a fundamentally risky business that requires real thought and care. In the process of removing barriers, there's a risk you remove some crucial safeguards too.

Let's do a deep dive on trading apps and figure out what the opportunities – and pitfalls – might be.

Going FAANGbusters

TRADING APPS LIKE Freetrade, Robinhood, Trading 212, Revolut, eToro, Invstr, Dabbl and Wombat aim to be fun, a doddle to use and cool.

They offer a direct and cheap route into what seem like the most promising investments in town. Unlike platforms, these apps shun the traditional world of active funds and, unlike robo-advisers, they positively encourage you to be your own fund manager.

They provide access to shares, ETFs and investment trusts, but on a more limited basis than traditional investment platforms. Some, like Invstr and Wombat, offer fractional trading, where you buy tiny slices of superstar shares, and the likes of eToro and Revolut even throw in cryptocurrencies, just to spice things up.

But it's the FAANGs that really drive interest in these apps. Tech titans get a shout-out on the 'Discover' tab of Freetrade's app and they routinely feature in the top ten stocks held by users. Invstr offers three 'fantasy portfolio' options tagged 'Tech Junkie', 'Sports Star' and 'Brand Swag'. Bitcoin, Apple, Amazon, Tesla, Netflix, Nike, Snap and gold all appear at least twice.

Revolut has a glimpse of a sample portfolio on its site featuring – surprise! – Apple and Facebook, saying its service means "being able to invest in the companies you love". Dabbl says it "allows you to invest in the brands and companies you love". I wonder what Wombat's slogan is… yep, it's "invest in brands you love".

Geez, we get the message! Trading can be trendy!

The lockdown trading bonanza

WELL, IT TURNS out share trading *has* become trendy. There was a huge jump in the number of young people buying and selling shares during the Covid-19 lockdown, both in the UK and US. All the established investing platforms benefited, but trading apps did particularly brisk business.

Between March and September 2020, Freetrade saw an 80% increase in new customers, with 27% aged from 18 to 25 and 42% aged from 26 to 35, while eToro saw a whopping 420% spike in the number of opened stock trades from January to June 2020, compared to the same period in 2019.[89]

Some of the reasons for this are obvious. We were stuck at home, bored, saving more and spending less: ideal conditions for a spot of trading. There were even reports that sports fans starved of live fixtures were getting their gambling thrill from trading instead.[90]

Younger people also became more aware of the economic climate and, despite all the doom and gloom, saw an opportunity. When stock markets plummeted in March 2020, it ended the stock market's longest-ever **bull run** – i.e. a period when share prices are rising – which suddenly made investments look cheap again.

Market analysts thought that the tech bubble would finally burst and shares in the FAANGs would fall back to more sensible levels. On the contrary: they surged to record highs and, alongside Tesla, were almost entirely responsible for the surprise comeback of the US stock market over the following six months.

This was partly down to over-reliance on technology during lockdown, but also because of enthusiastic personal investors, who made up 20% of all trading volumes in the US, according to a Bloomberg Intelligence report.[91] And helping to fuel the frenzy was Robinhood, an app that kicked off the freetrading craze in 2013 and had 13 million users at time of writing – three million more than at the end of 2019.

Robinhood's bizarre fandom

ROBINHOOD ATTRACTS A wild crowd. It's a world of macho and spontaneous traders who mock the sacred cows of investing and pile into individual shares to try and get rich quick – known as YOLOing.

They flock to brotastic and un-PC online communities like Reddit's 'WallStreetBets', which has more than a million members, and share eyebrow-raising memes, theories and stock tips. Young day traders have attracted millions of views on TikTok thanks to hashtags like #robinhoodstocks. One influencer even chose which shares to buy by picking tiles out of a Scrabble bag. Do NOT try that at home.

Robinhood investors have been responsible for lots of strange events in the US stock market. They snapped up shares in Hertz, a car rental company, *after* it went bankrupt in May 2020, in the hope that it would receive a government bailout. It didn't. They sent the share price of online services group Zoom Technologies soaring just after governments told people to work from home, but they confused it with Zoom Video Technologies, the popular video conferencing software.

And no prizes for guessing why shares in FANGDD Network Group – a small China-based real estate firm – did so well in spring 2020. It's because Robinhood investors were hunting down FAANG stocks. D'oh.

Investing: it's not a game

BUT THIS ISN'T funny. Investing in such a haphazard way can have devastating consequences. Alex Kearns, a 20-year-old student at the University of Nebraska, took his own life in June 2020 after he thought he'd racked up losses of $730,165 through Robinhood. Even more tragically, Alex misunderstood the nature of his investments, which were complicated options bets: he actually had $16,000 in his account. Alex's family have said they don't believe there were any other underlying reasons for his death, though it's important to stress this is a complex issue and we may never fully know why this happened. Please see the end of the chapter for further support and resources on mental health.

Robinhood's founders, Vlad Tenev and Baiju Bhatt, said they were "devastated" by the suicide. The company donated $250,000 to the American Foundation for Suicide Prevention, pledged to improve their educational resources and tightened eligibility requirements for anyone wanting to trade options.

From bright neon colours and giveaway stocks to the confetti that showers across the screen when you make your first trade, Robinhood has an addictive quality. This surely relates to the fact that the same part of the brain activated by drugs like cocaine also lights up when you anticipate a financial gain.[92]

I know what that feels like. Robinhood has cancelled its UK launch, but I downloaded the Freetrade app to give that a go. By getting a stocks and shares ISA for just £3 a month – with no charges on trades – I felt like I was beating the system. It was fun to go shopping for shares in their Discover tab, not least because they feature rad innovators like Tesla and well-known retail brands like Hotel Chocolat (officially described in Freetrade's spreadsheet of investments as "Posh Dairy Milk". Good one.).

And then when I tapped the 'buy' button, I became hooked. Waiting for my trades to go through, checking my investments every few hours, logging on as soon as I woke up… what was happening to me? You can find out how I overcame my Freetrade frenzy in my investing diary chapter later.

More seriously, though, research does suggest that young investors may be underestimating the effect that regular trading has on their mental health. Studies have even shown how traders who suffer large losses early in their careers can show symptoms of post-traumatic stress disorder.[93]

Insta investing

TO BE CLEAR, I like what Freetrade is trying to do: it's one of the more comprehensive and transparent trading apps on the scene. It does not offer options bets or any of the high-risk 'trading traps' I will discuss in chapter 15, and there is no suggestion that its users engage in riskier behaviour than other investors in the market: from what I know of Freetrade's community, they seem like a much more thoughtful, level-headed bunch than the reckless day traders seen stateside. It offers investments beyond the US and lots of investment trusts and ETFs too. There are plenty of 'boring' but potentially rewarding investments on there that you've never heard of, from healthcare firms to semiconductor producers.

I am all for cheap investing: Freetrade's general investment account has no fees and an ISA subscription is just £3 a month. If you don't mind having your trade done along with other customers' in bulk at 3 p.m. each day, that's free too. Compare this to £11.95 per trade at the biggest investment platform, Hargreaves Lansdown. Freetrade is clearly aimed just as much at serious investors who are sick of paying high trading charges as it is at novices.

But Freetrade offers a much greater selection of stocks behind a paywall of £9.99 a month. Plus, if you want to trade instantly in real time, so you know exactly what price you are buying at, it's £1 a trade.

Freetrade may offer news and an 'Invest Hub' on their website to try and educate people about investing (albeit in 'snackable' chunks of three to eight minutes). Great! But none of that is accessible through the app.

Kudos to Dabbl, which offers helpful information more directly through its app to help you make better investing decisions. But it still only offers the option to buy individual shares (though it does at least cover the UK as well as the US). There are three levels of access – the standard one being free to trade but with a £2.50 monthly admin fee. And I'll give a shout-out to Wombat for offering fractional trading in the UK. After all, America – contrary to what some navel-gazing US commentators would have you believe – is not the only investment market on the planet.

So, why do we have apps like Revolut and Invstr offering no access to stocks outside the US? Why are these apps nudging investors in the UK towards assets like cryptocurrency and gold, but not to any other kinds of investment?

Gambler's remorse

CLUES CAN BE found in an interview given by Invstr's founder, former merchant banker Kerim Derhalli. In a BBC Sounds podcast in 2020,[94] he said technology companies and cryptocurrencies are investments young people "feel they can own", citing Bitcoin as evidence that money can be made in a short period.

Such claims went unchallenged on the podcast, even though trying to make quick money through short-term investments is precisely what young people should *not* be doing.

Like many apps and websites, Invstr offers a fantasy portfolio and the chance to enter one of three competitive leagues with other fantasy investors to win prizes. Is it right to portray investing as a fun, dynamic game?

I am not against fantasy investing per se – it can be a useful way to flex your investing muscles with no consequences. But in November 2020, the top performers in its fantasy league table demo were shown as making gains of 27% in a month. I think this sets unrealistic expectations and may influence beginner investors to believe high, short-term gains are all that matter.

Invstr offers education through an 'Academy' where you can learn "everything you need to know about investing".

Once you are ready to do the real thing, the app acts as a gateway to a US platform called DriveWealth, where you can engage in fractional trading, but only in the US stock market, in dollars.

Revolut uses DriveWealth too, hence its exclusive focus on the US. The only other types of investment it offers are "crypto" and commodities.

I would argue that buying fractions of shares in US companies and/or picking up a few cryptocurrencies and commodities is *not* the way to begin your investing journey. You need to explore all the various options open to you, not be swayed by a few investments that *seem* to be guaranteed money-spinners.

The thought of making 27% a month is seductive. But if that's the reason you're investing, you've got it all wrong. As Moira O'Neill put it for the *FT*:

> Would you rather have £100 or a 50/50 chance at £200? If you take the £100, you're an investor. If you go all or nothing, you're a gambler. Put differently, would you rather put your money under your mattress or in an extremely volatile stock that could become worthless overnight or double in value? If you expect to double your money quickly, you are probably gambling, even if you are buying a well-known company on the London Stock Exchange rather than … playing blackjack in an online casino.[95]

Just because you can trade freely, and everyone on social media is piling in, doesn't mean you should follow the pack. In fact, it might just pay to keep a critical, questioning distance.

As for the FAANGs? Well, even they saw a sharp sell-off in September 2020, and the seemingly unstoppable Tesla fell 21% in one day. Ouch. It just shows, at the very least, that share trading is no smooth skyward ride. In fact, it could be a bucking bronco that throws you on your bum.

Stay cool!

INVESTORS IN THE US have always been into audacious share trading more than folks on this side of the pond (we prefer obsessing about property). Call it the American Dream on steroids.

Nonetheless, it looks like the Big Investing Game is taking off over here too. And whilst it's good take some risks, investing is not a game. As soon as you start seeing it that way, it's game over.

If you want a financial thrill, place a bet on Man United (on second thoughts, maybe not). If you want the chance to grow your money to fulfil goals and make a real impact with your investments, you've gotta have a proper investment strategy and act like a cool customer, not an adrenaline junkie.

You've got to be particularly wary about certain high-risk investments put forward by influencers and seemingly successful traders online. Let me explain why...

Investing and your mental health

Investing can be an intense experience, particularly when there are big movements in the markets and your portfolio. Be aware that this can affect your mental health and that there are proactive steps you can take to manage your thoughts and feelings around investing (see my last chapter for some helpful suggestions). However, if you have a history of or are currently dealing with mental health issues, it's vital that you seek clinical advice and start investing only if your GP and/or mental health practitioner says it is safe.

If you have been affected by the issues raised in this chapter, you can phone the Samaritans on 116-123, and more information can be found at mind.org.uk, samaritans.org and moneyandmentalhealth.org/get-help.

CHAPTER 16

The truth about investing influencers

"HOW I QUIT my job and ended up earning £100,000 a year investing!"[96]

This was an intriguing headline published in the *Daily Telegraph* in 2019. It concerned a chap called Jay Smith, who had nabbed a six-figure salary by the age of 30 by allowing other people to copy his investments.

Mr Smith is what you might call an investing influencer. In the past decade, we have seen legions of ordinary people become commercial powerhouses, generating huge incomes through brand partnerships and advertising – all thanks to the internet. And the once-exclusive world of investing certainly hasn't escaped the influencer trend.

There are all kinds of influencers operating in finance and investment today. We've touched on FIRE influencers, who evangelise about passive investing and income, and those who tip shares through hashtags like #invest on TikTok. There are also those who spread the word of cryptocurrencies, while others push complex stuff like spread betting and contracts for difference as a sure-fire route to riches.

There are also celebrities not known for their financial prowess, like former contestants on *Love Island*, passionately promoting forex trading – a topic that strangely never came up when they were playing Snog, Marry, Pie in the villa.

The internet is an amazing source of education, enlightenment and empowerment. But man, it's a jungle out there. The chance to copy successful traders may seem like a gift, but it can be a Pandora's box of risks too.

And while there are qualified, responsible investment influencers on social media, honestly sharing what they have learned, there are also many fraudsters selling nothing but bets with poor odds.

Let's evaluate investment influencers and see if what they advertise really stacks up.

Trading up: the eToro story

ONE SITE HAS capitalised heavily on the investment influencer concept and that's eToro. Founded in 2007 in Israel, it soon set itself apart from other platforms through two main features. Firstly, it was one of the few mainstream sites that allowed you to capitalise on the astonishing rise of **Bitcoin**, a cryptocurrency we'll explore in more detail in the next chapter, through something known as a **contract for difference (CFD)**.

As its name suggests, this is a contract between two parties, usually the 'buyer' and 'seller', promising that the buyer will pay to the seller the difference between the current value of an asset and its value at contract time. Likewise, if the difference is negative (i.e. the asset has lost value once the contract matures), the seller pays the buyer instead.

This particular method for 'doing' Bitcoin has now been banned by the financial regulator in the UK so if you want to trade Bitcoin or other cryptocurrencies, you have to directly own the asset through a third-party **digital wallet**, which eToro now offers.

The second innovation of eToro was to offer social trading – the ability to 'copy' successful investors' portfolios on the site and replicate their returns. And this is where Jay comes in.

He gets paid 2% commission by eToro on the total value of his followers' funds, *on top* of the returns he makes from his investments, a mix of shares and CFDs. The *Telegraph* story showcased other gurus who have thousands of 'followers' on the site, who between them have portfolios worth £8m.

You might be thinking: "Why don't I follow the likes of Jay on eToro, since they've clearly got the right idea?" Indeed, you might fantasise about going one step further and becoming an influencer yourself.

Beginners need not apply

On the surface, social trading seems democratic, cheaper and more efficient than traditional active funds. For instance, eToro talks of zero-commission trading on stocks and ETFs, no fees for copying star traders and an average annual profit of 29% on its 50 most copied traders in 2019. That compares to a typical return of 22% for active UK equity funds and 17% on FTSE 100 companies in the same year.[97]

While eToro's star traders are not professional fund managers, they have (to quote Liam Neeson in *Taken*) a very particular set of skills.

Popular traders on the site do tend to have a background in business and finance, possessing knowledge of trading concepts that would be beyond most people. They're also dedicated, giving up jobs or their spare time to research, trade and frequently update their followers. Beginners and hobbyists need not apply!

In a way, that's reassuring. These guys – and they are mostly men – don't seem that far off the paradigm of 'expert' fund managers to whom millions of investors entrust their money; and on certain short-term measures, they seem to be performing better too.

Looking under the bonnet

However, the devil is in the detail. There is a massive spectrum of investment strategies being pursued by traders on the site, with various levels of risk involved. Some higher-risk portfolios go up and down month-on-month, year-on-year, more than Dwayne Johnson's eyebrows.

Yet it's only their past 12 months of returns that are highlighted on eToro's 'Discover Traders' page, putting a huge emphasis on short-term performance. Is there a danger that new, inexperienced investors will hitch their wagon to those shooting the lights out one year, only to bail when they tank the next?

It can be difficult to pick out the most suitable traders to copy unless you know exactly what you're looking for and have a decent knowledge of investing yourself. While the site offers a now-standard quota of educational resources for all the normies out there, the whole process is certainly not as straightforward as saying "goojibooboo" – which is what eToro's goofy online ads, featuring Alec Baldwin, would have you believe.

The three trading traps to avoid

SO FAR, I have tried to be balanced about the investment choices available to young people today, outlining all their pros and cons. However, I will categorically say NONE of the following options are appropriate for young investors starting out.

Forex

This is a portmanteau of 'foreign currency' and 'exchange', often referred to as foreign exchange or FX. We have all used foreign exchanges to convert our money into other currencies for travel purposes, but forex traders try to profit from the differences in currency pricing. In the past, this was done primarily through **forex brokers**, who would buy and sell currencies through a forex trading platform. But online trading has given rise to **derivative** products, where investors can cheaply 'track' the underlying currency market rather than buy and sell the currencies through a third party. There are two main ways to track currency markets, which you'll often hear mentioned alongside forex but can be used to trade other assets, like shares and commodities. The first is…

Spread betting

Spread betting is where you literally bet on the future value of assets or financial markets. Not only can you bet that an underlying investment will rise in value – called going long – but you can also bet that an investment will *fall* in value – called going short. If your bet is correct, your profits are calculated on how much the market or asset has moved in your favour. The second main form of derivative trading is…

Contract for difference

As explained above, a CFD is an agreement to exchange the difference in the price of an asset or market from when you 'opened' your position (i.e. bought it) to when you 'closed' it (i.e. sold it).

How do 'commission-free' platforms make their money?

Commission-free platforms like Trading 212 and FreeTrade are planning to make money by growing their customer base through free stock trading before moving to a subscription or so-called 'freemium' model, where users have to pay to upgrade to a better package. But Trading 212, as well as eToro, partly rely on making money from **spreads** – that is, the difference between the buying and selling price of investments. The profits on CFDs and cryptocurrencies are likely to be an important part of that. Platforms must now prominently disclose and explain the chances of losing money on CFDs on their homepages following a regulatory crackdown. But still, it's worth bearing in mind that some business models in this sector do appear to rely partly on the sale of higher-risk investments.

Betting with poor odds

I HAVE ONLY provided a broad definition of forex, spread betting and CFDs because, frankly, I don't want you getting any ideas. The European Securities and Markets Authority says between 74% and 89% of retail investors lose money trading in forex markets. The chance of losses on CFDs and spread betting is usually between 75% and 90%. Derivative trading primes investors to be speculative, to focus on the short term and push all their chips towards a few spots on the roulette table. We know this is the antithesis of effective investing. Young people should be thinking long term, and investing in an informed and cool-headed way in a variety of assets to spread their risk.

More generally, trading sites frequently offer demo accounts to help you practice investing; but play-acting is a very different state of mind compared to having actual money at stake, which can cause traders to take fright and make poor decisions. This is one reason why investors lost more than £1 billion trading CFDs in 2018, according to the FCA. That figure is likely to have been even higher in recent years amid faster-moving, uber-volatile markets.

The biggest high-risk factor in all this is **leverage**, where you only put down a fraction – called a **margin** – of the trade you're making, with the provider loaning you the rest. This allows traders to gain larger exposure to markets and amplify gains. But it also compounds losses because you're essentially borrowing to invest.

It's easy to move from plain-vanilla share trading into CFDs on eToro. When you buy shares, you're automatically presented with the option to buy twice or five times as much using leverage. Should you choose that, it states underneath that it's a CFD trade and that "higher leverage means higher risk" – but you would need to remember, at that point, that the higher risk specifically means that the chance of losing money with CFDs is 75% to 90%.

What about copy trading? Jemima Kelly on the *FT* Alphaville blog[98] has argued copy trading "is more often than not CFD trading" – and even when it isn't, it can *become* CFD trading without followers being fully aware. She wrote:

> The copier starts by being given the exact same positions as the person they have decided to copy (let's call them the copyee), whether those be long or short, and leveraged or unleveraged. It means if the copyee then decides to dial up the risk at some point and add some leverage to their positions, that leverage is also added to the copier's positions, without warning or even notification (and vice versa, if the copyee de-risked). So, it's pretty easy for a copier to suddenly be exposed to a significant amount of added risk, without necessarily knowing it.

All these risks are flagged up in eToro's General Risk disclosure and section on copy trading risks. Would-be investors are taken through an in-depth questionnaire when they open an account, asking them how much financial experience they have and what their assets, earnings, goals, expectations and employment status are.

It's possible to copy traders who stay away from leverage and are seeking to manage their risks as responsibly as possible. Anyone interested in copy trading needs to do a serious amount of what the business world would call 'due diligence' before they jump in.

Insta-perfect

NOW, IT'S FAIR to say I'm no fan of forex, CFDs and spread betting. So, why are they plastered all over social media? Pre-internet, advertising was a far more select and controlled affair. Only the biggest, most established companies had the opportunity and budget to build brand awareness. They used a select tier of A-list celebrities to endorse their products. Their only outlets were TV, newspapers, cinema, magazines, billboards and mailouts.

Today, anyone with some presentational flair can make *themselves* a valuable brand. Thanks to social media, you can build your own audience by projecting a desirable lifestyle, useful advice, inspirational wisdom, or a sexy image.

You can monetise that following by selling your own products and services or promoting third parties, either by getting paid upfront or by earning commission from click-throughs. Sites like Instagram have a compulsive appeal, visual potency and direct reach that equates to marketing gold.

Social media advertising has been a godsend for millions of useful small businesses and talented entrepreneurs, especially those who are left behind by traditional employment. So long as influencers are transparent about their commercial behaviour, it's all good, clean fun.

Likewise, if grown adults can be 'influenced' into blowing their cash on harmless tat, then hey, that's their prerogative.

But influencer culture is now being married to high-risk investments, fuelling an illegal industry that's ruining young people's finances. At time of writing, Instagram had over 14 million posts with the hashtag #forex. Here's the truth behind most of them. (FYI – Instagram influencers are distinct from the copy traders I was discussing above. Copy traders are not doing anything illegal – they are legitimate, often experienced investors. They belong in a completely different category to the people I am about to discuss.)

Smooth criminals

Individuals post pictures of sports cars, designer handbags, lavish houses and luxury holidays, which they claim to have bought with cash earned from trading foreign currency. They urge followers to sign up for expensive courses that will teach them how to make it rain. Their snake oil is 'signals': supposedly accurate, informed tips on how to trade forex.

It's bullshit – and illegal bullshit at that. These influencers are not regulated or qualified to offer investment advice. Their claims about how much you can earn are completely bogus and they never tell you what the risks are. Their wealth, if genuine, is made purely from selling fake signals or commission earned when they persuade people to sign up to third-party trading sites, which don't seem to care that their 'affiliates' are recruiting new customers under false pretences.

Worse still, scammers have shamelessly exploited the Covid-19 crisis, luring in desperate young people who have lost jobs or income with promises of pots of gold at the end of the forex rainbow.

These silver-tongued charlatans also pay celebrity 'friends', usually famous because of reality TV or modelling, to vouch for their services. Do these celebrities with thousands or millions of followers know or understand they are endorsing illegal behaviour? That's unclear. Many quietly delete the offending posts after journalists expose the criminal practice behind them.

In 2019, UK fraud authorities warned that hundreds of Instagram users aged between 20 and 30 had been conned by the promise of high returns, losing nearly £9,000 each on average. One victim in his 20s, Oliver Broadbent, bravely spoke to the *Times* after losing £1000 (on three losing bets worth £350) to a forex influencer in 2019. He said:

> That £1,000 felt like £10,000 at that time in my life. It was all my savings I had held on to for years from birthdays and Christmas.

How has this been allowed to happen? The FCA says it can only deal with misleading promotions if they're undertaken by regulated firms, though critics believe it should and can go further to prosecute those flouting the law. The best the FCA has done (so far) is flag up illegal accounts on their website.

Frustratingly, there would be far tighter regulation of this whole area if it were reclassified as gambling, as influencers would be forbidden from advertising these 'bets' as investment opportunities. But that would require a legal change and, despite pressure from campaigners, the government has no plans to change course at time of writing. I just hope it doesn't take more young people to lose money – or worse – before the government changes its mind.

In the meantime, here are all the warning signs that you're dealing with a Wolf of Instagram – because it's not just your Nana who's vulnerable to crooks…

- They're recommending a forex, CFD or spread betting product without fully stating the risks.
- They're selling 'signals' through a course or monthly subscription model.
- They're guaranteeing big returns (i.e. thousands of pounds) in a short space of time with high or 100% success rates on their signals.
- Their posts look like stills from a Cardi B music video or they use stereotypical imagery associated with high finance (e.g. graphs on screens).
- They aren't on the FCA's register of authorised firms (register.fca.org.uk).
- They operate solely through social media (e.g. you can only contact them by DM on Instagram).
- They don't have any reviews through a credible review website that relate to the service they offer (celeb endorsements don't count).
- A quick Google search shows up negative reviews or mainstream press criticism about their dodgy practices.

If an influencer is promoting a third-party product or service, they should declare if they are being paid, and if so, include the hashtag #advert (or any clear variation of it). Any post that doesn't do this can be reported to the Advertising Standards Authority.

If you suspect you've encountered a Wolf of Instagram, please report them to the FCA at fca.org.uk/consumers/misleading-financial-adverts/report.

Hopefully, you have started to get the measure of the Great Investing Internet and how you can avoid tumbling too far down its overwhelming, occasionally ruinous rabbit hole.

But before I move onto discussing the likely pillars of your investing strategy, there's one more issue we need to deal with: the Bitcoin bandwagon. Should you jump on?

CHAPTER 17

Bitcoin: a bit problematic

WE ALL KNOW the dreaded 'fear of missing out'. And today, nothing represents investing FOMO quite like Bitcoin. In a way, cryptocurrency has become the Pied Piper of money, enticing young people away from a flawed economic system into a cave of financial wonders, filled with (seemingly) guaranteed riches. Who wants to be the little kid left behind in the town with all the stupid adults?

This book can't cover all the ins and outs of cryptocurrency. But there's no way I could ignore it.

Here, I'll strip away the mystique surrounding Bitcoin and give you the facts. You need to be hard-headed and informed rather than allowing yourself to be lured to that dark crypto cave at the sound of a banging tune.

FYI, I deal only with Bitcoin in this chapter because it's complicated enough without throwing another 2000 less established cryptocurrencies into the mix.

Let's get to it.

The crypto craze begins

BITCOIN WAS FOUNDED on the belief that national currencies are being dangerously devalued by central banks, which have faced pressure from governments to keep printing digital money to buy assets like government bonds. This has become the default strategy to stimulate economies following crises like the 2008 financial crash and Covid-19 (see chapter 1).

Currency sitting inside these state-based, legal frameworks is often seen as having no intrinsic value, only what governments and citizens can *agree* is its value. This is known as **fiat** money. Bitcoin believers argue that fiat money will inevitably be corrupted by governments, like the bolivar notes in Venezuela that have more value as craft paper than as functional currency.[99] This helps to explain why Venezuela, a once-prosperous country that has largely collapsed, has one of the highest rates of Bitcoin adoption in the world.[100]

An unknown character (or group of people) going by the name of Satoshi Nakamoto came up with Bitcoin in 2009. It was named **cryptocurrency** because crypto means 'secret' or 'hidden', an apt description for this submarine-esque currency swimming under the surface of government control and regulation.

Individual bitcoins can only be digitally **mined** by those with access to masses of supercomputers that can solve elaborate mathematical codes. So no, you can't mine a few on your lunchbreak using your trusty Apple Mac.

There is a finite number – 21 million – which won't be fully mined until 2140. Bitcoin production is programmed to slow down and become more difficult over time. In theory, this should make Bitcoin more valuable in the long run.

The **miners** also help to verify and update transactions on the **blockchain**. This is a kind of digital register on which every single Bitcoin transaction is recorded, and miners are directly rewarded with Bitcoin for their efforts. Rather than have banks or other institutions oversee the blockchain, Bitcoin users deal directly with one another in what's known as a **peer-to-peer** network.

The only information publicly viewable on this blockchain is the **address** of individual Bitcoin accounts. Those addresses are a random string of 26 to 35 letters and numbers, so (again, theoretically) that makes transactions impossible to trace back to individuals.

Too cryptic by half

THAT IS AN extremely basic description of how cryptocurrency works. But I'm just not sold on it. Here's why.

Firstly, people who believe in Bitcoin tend to be committed **libertarians**, driven by the pursuit of individual freedom and opposed to government intervention of any sort. They have an unhealthy degree of certainty about how governments and central banks are destined to ruin our finances. Fiat money, despite its flaws, keeps working because it's based on widespread trust and co-operation: two essential ingredients for any kind of commerce or prosperity.

Extreme Bitcoin fans don't like to acknowledge the need for vital checks and balances, like your bank's ability to alert you (and the authorities) when they see suspicious transactions on your account. There are reasons why we have regulations, laws, and oversight when it comes to something as important as money.

There's so much about cryptocurrency that's confusing, illogical, and unproven. For instance, advocates say the radical transparency of the blockchain could clean up the world of money once and for all.[101] Sure, blockchain technology itself could prove very useful in the future (though we don't know for certain). But how come, so far, it's been a haven for criminals, who love to use cryptocurrency for money laundering?[102] It's estimated that nearly half – 46% – of Bitcoin transactions are related to illegal activity.[103]

A lot of people promoting or using Bitcoin just don't give a monkey's about the principles behind it. They're either looking to make a quick buck, hide their ill-gotten gains or defraud people. There are many crooks who have exploited the complexities and underground nature of cryptocurrency.

The most famous example is Ruja Ignatova, the so-called "Missing Crypto Queen" who was the subject of a recent hit podcast of the same name.[104] Presenter Jamie Bartlett and his team charted how Ignatova and her cronies orchestrated a global scam under the guise of a fake cryptocurrency called One Coin, conning £100m out of UK investors alone. Victims were swindled through a toxic brew of social media, slick multi-level marketing and word of mouth from manipulated friends/family. Incredibly, many still believe their 'investments' will come good, attacking journalists and fellow victims who are publicising the truth.

The not-so-wonderful world of Bitcoin

FURTHERMORE, BILLIONS OF pounds worth of Bitcoin have been stolen by criminals who have hacked into dozens of **trading exchanges** (or **platforms**) where people buy and sell their cryptocurrencies. Such large-scale heists can cause sharp falls in the value of Bitcoin.[105]

Many people have also had their entire stash stolen from **wallets**, which are web-based stores for people's Bitcoin. These casualties are often knowledgeable experts, like technology writer Monty Munford[106] and Bitcoin champion Dominic Frisby.[107] If even they can fall through the Bitcoin trapdoor, what hope is there for the rest of us?

It's clear the "wonderful world" of Bitcoin as described by companies like eToro doesn't *quite* match up to the reality.[108]

Here's why I won't be moving to Planet Bitcoin any time soon.

Bitcoin's rise can't be compared to other investments

Sure, the growth of Bitcoin has outstripped that of other assets in recent times. One analysis found Bitcoin topped the investment league table in the five years leading up to 31 October 2019, with a cumulative return of more than 3000%. That compares to just 78% for developed market equities and 73% for property (assets we'll describe in more detail soon).[109]

But you're comparing apples with pears. Bitcoin was only established in 2009 and didn't really catch on until the mid-2010s. Prior to that, it was only valued in the low dollars. Many markets have quickly rocketed in value in the past, from tulips to Beanie Babies.[110] (Ah, I remember the Beanie Baby craze well…)

What counts is how positive and stable the **fundamentals** are. These are the underlying characteristics of the investment that tell us how valuable it might be in the future. And Bitcoin's fundamentals are flimsy AF.

The future value of Bitcoin is completely unknown

No investment comes with guaranteed returns. But you can use a range of tried-and-tested measures to decide how promising the fundamentals look. For instance, shares can be assessed on a

price-to-earnings ratio, where you compare a company's share price to the company's earnings per share. That way, you might be able to spot a firm that's undervalued, with a low share price yet solid earnings.

There aren't any credible ways to measure Bitcoin's future potential. That's because while we have loads of info on the *supply* of Bitcoin, it's harder to know what's driving *demand*. But it looks an awful lot like the kind of greedy speculation that made Bongo the Monkey and other Beanie Babies the hottest investment in the playground for a few years.

Don't believe me? In October 2020, our old friend the FCA banned the sale of cryptocurrency derivatives – i.e. products tracking the price of cryptocurrencies – to consumers like you and me, saying there was "no reliable basis for the valuation" of cryptos, among other reasons.[111]

Bitcoin is extremely volatile – more so than other assets

Rampant speculation is making Bitcoin extremely volatile. It soared to $20,000 (£15,800) in December 2017, after doubling in a fortnight. But in 2018 its value fell more than 70%. Between 2014 and 2017, cryptocurrencies were more volatile even than currencies in the least developed countries in the world – with Bitcoin being the most topsy-turvy.[112]

Greta wouldn't like Bitcoin!

If you're passionate about making your investments eco-friendly, Bitcoin might not be a great shout.[113] There are around four million computer rigs worldwide dedicated to the problem-solving lottery of mining, that ends up being lucrative for just

2% of them.* The other 98% never hit the jackpot and have an average lifespan of just one and half years before they're rendered obsolete by a new generation of whizz-bang machines.

As Alex de Vries – a blockchain specialist at PwC – puts it,[114] these also-rans will operate:

> pointlessly for a few years, using up energy, and producing heat, and then … just get trashed because they can't be repurposed. It's insane.

Safety is far from guaranteed

Investment losses are one thing. Having your money stolen, with no access to compensation, is another. Many hold their Bitcoin in **hot wallets** (that is, connected to the internet) opened through crypto exchanges, which are routinely hacked. But you are still vulnerable if you open a hot wallet via software on your phone or PC and keep it there instead.

Even if you take the extra step of opening a **cold wallet**, which you keep offline in an external hard drive or USB stick, you're not out of the woods. How will you make sure it doesn't get lost or nicked? And you'll still need to securely store your **private key**, a secret code that is impossible to memorise (it's 256 characters long!) which allows you to spend, send and sell your Bitcoin. It turns out the only safe thing to do is to write the code on that prehistoric thing called a piece of paper. And if you lose that, you're screwed.

* Successful miners receive Bitcoin supposedly worth £4.6bn each year.

Cryptocurrency isn't being depicted accurately online

The online conversation surrounding Bitcoin isn't always honest and balanced. According to the FCA, as many as a third of people who have bought cryptocurrencies in recent times did so in response to advertising.[115] Yet the Cryptoassets Taskforce found in 2018 that crypto promotions are "not typically fair or clear and can be misleading".[116]

It also found that people who buy into cryptocurrencies after seeing advertising are less likely to understand the risks involved (such as the lack of regulation) and more likely to regret their decision. The FCA will now be given extra powers to crack down on this advertising boom, but good luck trying to regulate the lawless wilds of social media.

Cryptocurrency can be a Trojan horse for fraud

In the 2018–2019 financial year, Britons officially lost at least £20 million to cryptocurrency fraud (though the true figure is much higher, as many losses simply aren't reported). Many scammers falsified endorsements from influencers like Martin Lewis, founder of MoneySavingExpert.com. Mr Lewis has faced a (so far) fruitless battle to eliminate these posts from social media, which have conned many followers out of thousands of pounds.[117]

Worse still, some celebrities have *genuinely* backed new cryptocurrencies that have turned out to be scams. For instance, boxer Floyd Mayweather was paid $100,000 and DJ Khaled $50,000 to endorse a new cryptocurrency spending card which turned out to be fraudulent. Both were fined a combined $767,500 by the US financial regulator.

Crypto investors aren't necessarily smart Alecs

All the Bitcoin bros – 79% of UK crypto investors are male, after all[118] – would have you believe the train is leaving the station and you're not on it. But research produced for the Think Forward Initiative (a Europe-wide financial literacy movement)[119] showed that the more financially literate you are, the *less* likely you are to invest in Bitcoin. Far from being smart Alecs who are on to a good thing, researchers Georgios Panos and Tatja Karkkainen said a "large" number are "unsophisticated investors with lower financial literacy". They added:

> These investors are likely to overestimate the reward prospects in cryptocurrencies and underestimate the risk involved. … For any new financial instrument or alternative asset to become established, less volatile, and less likely to be subject to manipulation, the market needs to be dominated by sophisticated investors and legitimate users. Our evidence and the recent evidence regarding the uses of the bitcoin suggests that the current state of the market for cryptocurrencies is far from that.

The financial blogger Mr Money Mustache, aka Pete Adeney, has retired early (see part 1's bonus chapter) – but not thanks to Bitcoin. He's against it for moral as well as practical reasons. He makes the distinction between owning useful assets that "create products, services or cashflow" with social value, and speculating purely to make profits. The latter, he writes, is a "win-lose battle against other humans with money as the sole objective". He goes on to say:

> Bitcoin is only valuable if it truly becomes a critical world currency. In other words, if you truly need it to buy stuff, and thus you need to buy coins from some other person in order to conduct important bits of world commerce that you can't

do any other way. Right now, speculators are the only people driving up the price.

A speculative cult currency like bitcoin is only valuable when you cash it out to a real currency, like the US dollar, and use it to buy something useful like a nice house or a business. When the supply of foolish speculators dries up the value evaporates – often very quickly.[120]

Turning FOMO into JOMO!

SO, IT'S TIME to turn Bitcoin FOMO into JOMO (the joy of missing out!) and be thankful that you're not tying up your money in such an unknown, volatile, and often dangerous escapade.

I don't want to write off cryptocurrency's ability to help the unbanked (i.e. those without access to conventional banking), and blockchain could yet become a disruptive power for good.

But it's clear that Bitcoin is deeply problematic. It's being treated far more as a get-rich-quick scheme than as a functional currency: you only need to pop down to your local chippy and ask if they accept Bitcoin to find that out.

Plus, Bitcoin's gains rely purely on being able to sell your currency for more than you paid for it, as opposed to investing in companies conducting useful activities with social value. The *Own It* philosophy is not about profiteering for its own sake: it's about having a stake in the real economy so you can drive positive change, both in your life and in the wider economy.

With that said, let's look at what you can invest in to help you achieve just that.

CHAPTER 18

Understanding classic assets

NOW IT'S TIME for us to look at what you can invest in as you build your portfolio. Remember, your portfolio is your overall collection of investments.

Even if you end up choosing ready-made portfolios from robo-advisers and platforms, or investing in active or tracker funds, you still need to understand what's happening inside these investments.

We need to think about what is most likely to end up in your portfolio by looking at the individual investment building blocks known as **asset classes**. These are the various categories of investment that each have their own characteristics.

Asset classes are like the individual Lego pieces that make up your portfolio. You need to grasp what they are and how they connect together before you can build the investing equivalent of, say, the Millennium Falcon (don't worry, creating a portfolio is *way* more straightforward – and less plasticky).

In this chapter, I will introduce the main asset classes of shares, bonds, property and commodities, including gold. In chapter 19 I move on to the more exotic asset classes. And then in chapter 20, we'll talk about what kind of investment strategy you could adopt. Ah, it's all coming together nicely!

Taking your share

I'VE WANGED ON about **shares** (also known as **stocks** and **equities**) a lot in the book already. But they will be an important part of your investing journey, because of the long-term growth potential they offer.

In case your memory needs jogging, shares are issued by companies that **list** (or **float**) on the stock market. This process is known as an **initial public offering** (IPO). It's also commonly described as 'going public'.

IPOs happen when firms want to scale up and raise money beyond the private sources of funding that got their business off the ground. It's also a way to reward those early investors, who exit with a huge payday at the point of an IPO. Going public allows companies to access a far larger body of investors, from you and me right up to **institutional investors** – e.g. the fund managers taking care of our pensions.

Each individual share in a company has a value: this is the company's **share price**. Each share is a small part of ownership of a public company. For example, if a company has issued 100 shares and you own one of those shares, you own 1% of the company. In reality companies issue many millions of shares. Shares are traded throughout each working day, with their price fluctuating based on supply and demand.

Companies list on a particular stock exchange (or multiple exchanges across the world) based on the total value of all their shares, known as their **market capitalisation (market cap)**. If a company has issued one million shares and its share price is £1, the market capitalisation of the company – the total value of all its shares – is £1 million.

The market cap is often usefully abbreviated when referring to the comparative value of companies. The most well-known categories are **large cap**, **mid cap** and **small cap**, but you also get **mega caps** like Apple right down to **micro caps** and even **nano caps**, with a total market capitalisation of less than £50m.

For example, Britain's largest cap companies list on the FTSE 100 index, but there is also the FTSE 250 and 350, encompassing the next biggest companies. The FTSE All-Share index lists all companies trading on the **London Stock Exchange**.

Many of the best-known companies in the UK – such as Tesco, easyJet and Barclays, to name just three – are listed on the London Stock Exchange and anyone can buy shares in these companies to own a small part of them.

As soon as a company goes public, its ass is owned by shareholders. It must file a comprehensive, independently verified account of its financial position every six months (known as its **results**). A public company is at the mercy of the markets: companies having a moment could see their share price soar, but equally, a **profit warning** (i.e. a notice that profits will be lower than previously forecast) could cause a company's share price to plunge.

Companies have to publish any information that is **price-sensitive** in a statement to the stock exchange. Results will usually be released at 7 a.m., before the market opens. In November 2020 two of the big companies producing vaccines for Covid-19 – Pfizer and Moderna – were criticised for releasing significant trial results in the middle of a trading day, which was highly unusual.

Many smaller and younger UK companies choose to list on the **Alternative Investment Market (AIM)** because it is cheaper and less onerous for them to do so. For investors, AIM shares tend to be at the racier end of the risk menu, but AIM does feature many solid medium-sized companies too. Bear in mind that investing in AIM companies is for active investors who are buying shares in individual companies only: tracking the AIM through an index fund is not recommended.

Owning It, redefined

It's not compulsory for a company to go public. But share ownership can be a beautiful thing, folks. It should make companies accountable, transparent, and more effective.

Investors have the right to challenge anything they don't like (such as fat cat salaries or environmental abuse) and put pressure on a company to change course. Ordinary shareholders can kick up a fuss at the **annual general meetings** (these are town hall gatherings hosted by companies), while big investors can summon chief execs to have a lil' talk. This surely is the crux of 'owning it': using your investment power to drive positive change.

Unfortunately, as we saw in chapter 9 with pensions, neither individual nor institutional investors have fully done their bit. Too often, executives have been allowed to reward themselves for failure and get away with bad behaviour, like destroying precious environmental habitats or paying workers peanuts. This stalls progress and corrodes trust in a system that would work much better if everyone was stepping up to the plate.

Thankfully, there are **activist investors** out there who trigger change, like forcing lousy CEOs to step down or getting firms to decarbonise. You can be one of them: see chapter 10 on woking up your pension. If the companies you invest in are bang out of order, tell them. This is one area where 'cancel culture' might actually do some good.

Whenever you invest, particularly if you decide to become a stock picker, always remember that you are becoming a shareholder, first and foremost. If your chosen companies make you feel embarrassed – even ashamed – rather than proud, it may be time for a rethink.

Why the price isn't *always* right

A whole heap of factors can influence the share price of a company, from the concrete (its latest results) to the abstract (do people even *like* Facebook anymore?).

But when a company first goes public, how does it value itself? Well, it decides how many shares to issue and then a nominated investment bank will calculate a market valuation, based on stuff such as likely demand for shares, recent profits, and growth prospects.

Now, a highly valued IPO could genuinely be worth it, L'Oréal style. To some extent, companies going public need to fake it till they make it, talking themselves up so they can inspire investment that will make their vision a reality. There have been some spectacular IPOs in recent times where shares have instantly shot up, like Trainline and The Hut Group.

But in recent years, we've seen IPOs with a level of hype that makes Hollywood marketeers look shy and retiring. WeWork, the co-working company with beer on tap, was due to list on the stock market in 2019. After its IPO plans went public, people started asking questions about the $47bn valuation of the company (it lost $1.9bn in 2018), its business model (why did it call itself a tech company when it was leasing out office space?) and its CEO Adam Neumann, who seemed to model himself on a terrifying combo of Jesus, Jeff Bezos and Liam Gallagher.[121]

Sure enough, WeWork's IPO collapsed and Neumann was ousted (albeit with a $1.6bn payout). It has become the ultimate cautionary tale of corporate hubris. There are many examples of private companies valued at more than a billion dollars/pounds – known as **unicorns** – whose actual performance as public companies fails to live up to their narrative, including Uber,

SmileDirectClub and Peloton (though the counterargument would be: give them time).

Free-trading apps often alert their customers to the hottest new IPOs available: I get notifications on my phone whenever a new one drops, like it's a new YouTube video. And who doesn't love a unicorn?

But perhaps it's a clue that a company's story is mythical, one that the kids love but the grown-ups know isn't actually real. Watch out for any company where, in the words of *Top Gun*'s Captain Stinger, its ego may be writing cheques its body can't cash. Find out what independent media commentators and analysts say before you invest.

Dividends R Us

I haven't mentioned **dividends** before now, but they are kinda a big deal.

A dividend is shiny bait offered by companies to encourage investors to stay in the game – namely in the form of a payout of so many pence per share, usually every half-year, in an **interim dividend** and a **final dividend**.

For example, if a company announces a dividend of 5p per share and you own 100 shares, you will receive a dividend payment of £5 (5p x 100 = 500p).

Most companies pay dividends twice a year, but some pay annually, quarterly or monthly. To receive each dividend a share must be **on the register** (bought) before an **ex-dividend** date published in advance by the company. Its shares will usually fall on that date and will be marked in listings as **XD**. So to qualify for the next dividend you must buy before the XD date.

Not every company pays dividends though – some companies are growing and reinvesting their spare cash (rather than paying it to investors as a dividend) and some companies might not have enough spare cash to pay a dividend.

If you are investing in a company because it pays a dividend, always check its **dividend cover**. Cover of 1.0 means the company's earnings exactly cover the dividend payout. Below 1.0 means the dividend is probably too high and may at some point be cut. Investors are happy when cover is somewhere between 1.1 and 1.5.

Shares often offer a double win – **capital growth** (i.e. a rise in their share price) over time AND dividends. Moreover, those receiving dividends have a choice: they can either take the cash or reinvest it to buy more shares of the company.

Dividends can make a big difference to your overall returns. In 2016, the FTSE 100 index of the UK's 100 biggest companies went up 14.4%. In the same year, the 100 companies paid an average dividend of 3.65%. If you add that 3.65% to the 14.4%, that's an overall return of more than 18%. Even in 2018, when the FTSE 100 index dropped 12.5%, the companies paid an average dividend of 4.3%, which cushioned the blow.

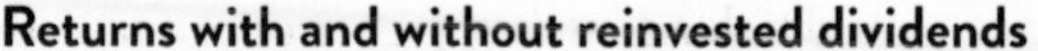

Returns with and without reinvested dividends

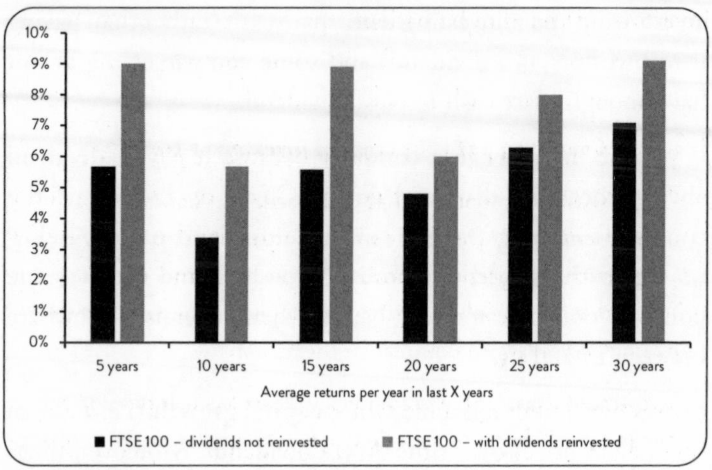

Source: AJ Bell

If you buy a passive index fund (see chapter 12) that tracks a London Stock Exchange index, it should reinvest the dividends from those companies, pay them out in income, or give you a choice.

Shares have a **dividend yield** at any given time, which depends on the latest share price. It's worked out by dividing annual dividends by the share price. If you buy a share at 100p and the past dividend was 5p a share, you should get a 5% return over a year – buying it at a 5% yield. If you buy the same share at a price of 50p, you are buying at a 10% yield. The current yields of shares are often shown in factoids when you look up a company.

Dividends are a massive part of UK investing culture: older investors in particular gravitate towards this **equity income** space, but who doesn't love a lil' bit of regular income? So it was pretty devastating to see three-quarters of UK companies cutting or cancelling dividends at the height of lockdown in 2020, as they couldn't rationalise payouts to investors amid falling revenues and the need for government support. But dividends have been slowly ticking back up, so income-focused investors just need to be patient.

Could you put your trust in investment trusts?

One investment option that you need to consider is the **investment trust**. This is a company that lists on the London Stock Exchange and its business is to invest in other companies. You can buy and sell shares in the investment trust just like buying and selling shares in any other company.

Investment trusts have traditionally been a small part of the market, partly because they don't pay commission to advisers or platforms to drive sales. But since these backhanded payments became taboo, trusts have gained a lot more ground: they now feature prominently on platforms and in the media. To be honest, I have always had a soft spot for them. Here's why:

- They often have cheaper management charges than mutual funds that do the same thing.
- They are companies with an independent board of directors. If the fund managers screw up, the board can go all Apprentice on them by firing them and appointing new ones. It doesn't happen very often, but enough to keep managers on their toes.
- Trusts can borrow money (popular in recent times when borrowing is so cheap) to invest extra cash in the market. This is a great strategy when markets are on the up; less so when they are in reverse. This borrowing to invest is called **gearing**.
- Trusts offer a way for you to spot undervalued investments that may flourish sooner or later. Trusts are valued day-by-day in relation to the value of their portfolios and tend to move roughly in line with them. But there is often a

gap. If the share price surpasses the value of the assets, this is known as a **premium**, whereas a share price that lags behind the value of its assets leads to a **discount**. That creates an opportunity for investors who get their timing right to make extra returns. In fact, there is a mini-industry of spreadsheet analysts and commentators out there calculating and reporting on the value of investment trusts. For those who can keep up with it, it makes for interesting and sometimes profitable reading. **Numis Securities** and **Winterflood Securities** are the big beasts in this field.

There are some downsides. Trusts can perform just as badly as other investment funds, though the board of directors won't tolerate underperformance for too long. Investment trusts can look expensive when they become popular and a rocketing share price has driven them to a big premium. Conversely, unloved, out-of-fashion trusts on wide discounts might never actually bounce back. There is also less information available on trusts than on funds, so you have to make a greater effort to seek out coverage, insight and information – but it could be worth your while.

The name's Bond

WHEN YOU HOLD equities, you are holding a tiny part of a company's capital, or equity. When you hold **bonds**, you are lending money to a company or a government, so you are a creditor holding a tiny part of their debt. For this you'll be paid a fixed rate, which makes bonds a less risky asset than equities.

Both equities and bonds are traded on the stock market; but while a share may or may not pay a regular dividend, a bond will guarantee to pay a fixed sum of money, known as the **coupon**. That rate may or may not be above the rate of inflation

– unless it is an **inflation-linked bond** (see chapter 1). Bonds will have a maturity date and the return is guaranteed if you hang on till the maturity date – but they can be bought and sold along the way.

Bonds are affected by external events, notably interest rates and the outlook for inflation. I don't recommend trying to understand how this works lest you burst a blood vessel.

Thankfully, bonds are graded pretty reliably by the markets, guided by brainbox economists, according to the risk of not getting your money back. The higher the risk, the higher the promised return. All the drama that has gone down in Greece and Venezuela in recent years means their bonds will pay a higher rate of interest than UK **gilts** or US **treasuries** (the individual names for national bonds).

Government bonds are much safer than company bonds, because a country is less likely to go bankrupt and default on its debts than a company. Government bonds come in three flavours – **short**, **medium**, and **long dated**.

Corporate bonds are debt issued by companies to fund their activities. For instance, Apple has borrowed over $50 billion from investors, and pays its bondholders 3%–4% a year. Corporate bonds that pay higher returns are classed as **high yield**, which means higher risk than **investment grade** bonds.

Providing the company (or government) doesn't go bust, a fixed payout at a certain point in the future is written in stone, usually the face value of the bond when issued. Even if a company runs into financial trouble, bondholders rank ahead of equity holders for repayment.

The return on a bond is known as the **yield**. The guaranteed payout on the bond is the **redemption yield**, while the return at any point along the way (as the bond price moves up or down) is the **running yield**.

Bonds are a time-honoured safety valve and can help to mitigate the more unpredictable risks of share investing. So, a more cautious portfolio usually has a higher concentration of bonds compared to shares.

In practice, for ordinary investors like you and me, investing in bonds is normally achieved through bond funds rather than buying bonds directly from the issuing government or company. Although bonds have traditionally been the classic **hedge** (i.e. means of protection) against the risks in equities, you may want to register the view of some experts that future economic trends will render bonds far less effective in that bodyguard-esque role. Or not! This is what investing is about: getting informed but being prepared to make your own call.

Hot property

I DISCUSSED INVESTING in property as a home in chapter 5. But you can invest in other bricks and mortar assets like office blocks, shopping malls, warehouses, and business parks. They produce a return from their rental income and they may also grow in capital value.

Property is like equities in having strong potential for growth, and like bonds in promising a steady income. But it can also spring big surprises, depending on the state of the property market and the economic cycle.

2020 saw much debate about how property funds would be affected by the move to working from home, leaving offices under-used. Funds investing more in big retail parks and in solid industrial parks, rather than town centre shopping hit by the pandemic, really came into their own.

So long as you are fully aware of the risks, property can be a valid part of any investor's portfolio. But it's better for investors to do this either directly as an owner or landlord, or through established funds. Investment trusts are the best bet here, because unlike mutual funds, they do not have to sell any assets to repay investors who want to leave the fund when the going gets tough. In 2009 and 2020, several mutual property funds were **gated** – i.e. temporarily closed – awaiting the market recovery, which meant investors could not exit. In an investment trust, you can always sell your shares.

Do NOT invest in property investment schemes promising blingy returns (between 6% and 10%). As of 2020, the Serious Fraud Office and police were investigating dozens of slick outfits which convinced investors to pay thousands of pounds upfront for luxury flats, hotels, care homes and student property which never got built and left many young investors nursing huge losses.[122] Remember a common theme of this book: something that seems too good to be true usually is.

Gold school

GOLD IS THE ultimate **safe haven**, meaning its value often soars when stock markets slump, as investors cling to a secure, tangible asset. It doesn't produce any interest or dividends and its price depends solely on demand and supply.

If you're a fan of heist movies, you'll think of gold as chunky bars that cost a fortune, housed in a bank vault with a fierce security set-up. But it's not as hard to own gold as you might think.

Royal Mint, which makes all our coinage, has a DigiGold service, where you own a slice of real gold stored in their vault for as little as £25. You can buy and sell your holding through its digital account at any time, with an annual management charge of 0.5%. You can also buy physical gold through traditional and online dealers (watch out for dealing and storage costs though).

You could also choose a specialist mining fund, run by experienced managers who pick from the range of global mining companies. But even a well-regarded fund like Blackrock Gold & General went from losses of 20% in 2015 to returns of 80% in 2016, so it's not all smooth sailing.

Another avenue is ETFs. They either track the gold price or buy physical gold. They have the advantage of low annual management costs and no stamp duty on purchases. Standing behind these shares are actual bars of physical gold held in secure vaults, providing you pick a **physical gold ETF**.

In 2020, Covid-19 sparked a goldrush, driving the price from just under $1500 an ounce at the start of the year to over $2000 by August, and gold ETFs were among the big winners.

Gold usually finds its way into most people's portfolios at one point or another. But gold's value is volatile and can be influenced by a changing outlook for the dollar, inflation, or the overall economy. So don't confuse the term 'safe haven' with 'these gold babies will buy me my first hot-tub next year'.

The commodities cosmos

FINALLY, THERE ARE lots of other **commodities** traded on global markets, from silver to soya beans (yum). They behave differently from other asset classes, so they help to diversify your portfolio and protect against inflation.

Commodities are the raw materials used to create the products we buy. They include wheat and cattle, oil and natural gas, gold and aluminium. There are also 'soft' commodities such as sugar, cocoa, and coffee – aka my diet as I near a deadline.

Their prices are linked not only to demand, but also to fundamental supply factors which can include weather, crop failure, or geopolitical instability.

Commodities have evolved with the development of **futures indices**, which reflect price expectations (i.e. what traders expect to happen in future), and new investment vehicles to track them. Again, you can buy ETFs covering a single commodity or a whole sector.

As with gold, you should look out for ETFs which genuinely invest in the physical commodities, not **synthetic ETFs**, which are financial instruments devised by banking smarty-pants but may not be all that reliable, as they don't actually invest in the underlying assets.

Commodities are by their nature a bit of a moving feast, so it's wise to limit your exposure to a smallish percentage of your investments. Just as I probably should limit my dietary exposure to Nescafé and Maltesers, eh?

Let's now move on to discussing miscellaneous assets that are at the more exotic end of the spectrum.

CHAPTER 19

Weighing up exotic assets

IN THE LAST chapter, we scoped out the main asset classes that will probably end up in your portfolio. But I also want to cover a few more alternative assets that may catch your eye, from start-up breweries and football shirts to – wait for it – song royalties. What a time to be alive.

Let's take a tour through the main kinds of investment exotica.

Collectible curiosities

SOME OF US justify buying, say, a luxury handbag by saying, "it's an investment!" This is not always totally spurious. Sure, we all secretly hope Nana will pass down a Ming vase that will make history on *Antiques Roadshow*. But there are other items that could become more valuable over time. These include:

- Vintage clothing
- Rare booze
- First editions of books
- Historic movie posters
- Certain musical instruments
- Arsenal's 'bruised banana' away shirt from the 1990s (no, I'm not making this up).

It requires, ahem, a certain character to hoard or hunt down these diamonds in the rough and keep them in pristine condition to sell at a future date. IMO, what's the point in having a passion for these things if you can never fully enjoy them?

Still, the 'performance' of certain collectibles is undeniable. A signed first edition of *Harry Potter and the Philosopher's Stone* went for £75,000 at auction in 2020.[123]

Never chuck out anything old without looking up if it might be valuable. Besides, collecting is a nice hobby, so try cultivating a specialism and having a regular root around your local charity shops and markets.

The P2P pickle

PEER-TO-PEER LENDING (often abbreviated to the funky-sounding **P2P**) is financial matchmaking: lending your money to businesses and individuals and giving you a fixed interest rate in return. P2P firms claim to cut out the banking middlemen to make loans cheaper and returns better.

The riskier the borrower, the higher your interest will be. But your cash is pooled with others and spread over a range of borrowers to soften the risk. Many P2P platforms also have a provision fund to cover defaults – i.e. people who fail to pay up.

Your rate should be paid in a fixed period, so the experience is akin to having a savings bond. But there is no guarantee you will be paid, and your money isn't covered by the Financial Services Compensation Scheme, so the real risks feel a lot more like investing.

People flocked to P2P in the 2010s because of dire interest rates and overpriced equities. Dozens of platforms exploded into life as would-be tech millionaires all launched their own pet ventures. Lenders were lulled into a false sense of security: after all, borrowers pay up just fine in normal times. But what happens when things get a bit dystopian, as they did in 2020?

Peer pressure

Platforms had long admitted that defaults would rise in a recession, with lenders receiving less money and/or waiting longer to get their cash back. Sure enough, in 2020 platforms slashed their rates and people started wondering if they would ever see their money again. The *Guardian* reported in October 2020 – seven months after the Covid-19 crisis hit – how one lender with Ratesetter was told she was 19,050th person in the queue for withdrawals.[124] I mean, Brits love queuing, but that's taking it too far.

This shows how P2P platforms can pose a problem in terms of **liquidity**. This is a key concept in finance, referring to how easily you can cash in your investments – or how 'liquid' they are. The Covid saga reminds us why you shouldn't put money you urgently need in investments that can become illiquid.

It also reinforces the importance of sticking to the big boys. The strongest platform proved to be Zopa – even if it had to cut its rate from 5% to 3% – largely because it was the only one that had been through the 2008 crash and learned how to survive. By contrast, we've had the collapse of platforms like Lendy and Funding Secure, with even the publicly listed Funding Circle posting some ropey financial results in recent years. The surviving P2P gang may bounce back from this crisis stronger than ever; only time will tell.

P2P can be a useful midpoint between the safe but pants interest on savings and the highwire risk and reward of investing. But you need to do your homework on key issues like liquidity and platforms' risk protocols.

Could you invest in Beyonce?

Fun fact! The Church of England (CoE) co-owns the rights to Beyonce's Single Ladies. So, every time that song gets streamed, played on the radio, or placed in a TV show or film, the CoE makes money off the royalties. Yass queen.

Hipgnosis is a new investment trust that snaps up the rights to popular songs and is one of the investments held in the CoE investment portfolio. Hipgnosis was set up by Merck Mercuriadis, a music industry bigwig who has managed acts like Elton John and Guns 'n' Roses. His rationale is that people will always want to listen to timeless tunes, whatever's going on: the number of Spotify users rose on average by 22% a month during the first 2020 lockdown.

So, if you like it, then you may want to put some kerching on it. But be aware that future returns rely on the continued growth of streaming, legal protections for copyright holders and Hipgnosis's portfolio being all killer, no filler.

Following the crowd

SO FAR, I have given the impression that the only way to buy into something you love, admire or at least think is a sound investment is through the stock markets. But these days, it's possible for anyone (not just venture capitalists) to back private companies at an early stage thanks to crowdfunding.

There are three main types of crowdfunding. There's **donation-based crowdfunding**, which is when individuals or organisations raise money from the public for a particular cause. An offshoot of this is **civic crowdfunding**, where you can help pay towards a community or public project. Backers receive no personal benefit, other than the warm glow of helping fellow human beings, of course.

Then there's **reward-based crowdfunding**, more commonly associated with passion projects like a podcast or indie film. Here, contributors get various tiers of perks, like merchandise and exclusive content. The bigger your contribution, the better your reward.

Finally, there's **equity crowdfunding**, which involves selling shares or bonds directly to the public. Investors should either receive income or benefit from the growth in their shares if the company or organisation does well. Civic crowdfunding can also fall under this umbrella via a **community share issue**.

Companies or organisations might crowdfund when they want to raise money on their own terms. Take Brewdog, the plucky, brash brewery from Aberdeen that seems hellbent on global domination. It's best known for its hipster bars spreading across the world, bad-ass brand, and controversial publicity stunts, like ironically issuing discounted pink bottles of beer to highlight the gender pay gap.

Daft punks?

But none of this would have happened without Brewdog's army of 'equity punks' who were mobilised into putting their money where their beermats were. In 2009, Brewdog pioneered a new breed of crowdfunding that fused attractive rewards (from t-shirts to beer fridges) with shares in the company. It went on to raise £79m and attract 145,000 investors, and at time of writing overshot its final-ever crowdfunding target of £7.5m.

But it's hard to know if Brewdog's backers are canny investors or just superfans who'll end up short-changed. Brewdog blossomed into a unicorn in 2017 when it sold a 22.3% stake of the business to US private equity giant TSG Consumer Partners and was valued at £1bn. On paper, this made a few thousand early 'punks' very wealthy but in practice, only 2% sold their shares,[125] and even then, they could only sell 15% of their stake.

Indeed, investors have had a pretty hard time cashing in their shares: their only real option is to sell them to one another on designated trading days. Moreover, the small print of the TSG deal dictated that the fat cats now rank above the punks in the event of any sale, stock market listing or liquidation – and will likely get a better price too.

In fact, Brewdog will have to be sold or publicly listed for at least £2.4bn to avoid ordinary shareholders seeing their stakes **diluted** (no pun intended), that is, reduced in value. In other words, it'll have to sell a LOT more booze very soon for shareholders to make any decent money. Given Brewdog lost more than £8m in the first six months of 2020, I'd keep the beers on ice for now.

The only reason to invest in Brewdog is to get some discounted ale because in my view, it's pretty unlikely you'll be toasting bumper investment returns in the future. And this is one of the more successful crowdfunding stories – wait till you hear about the flops…

Crowd crashes

There's Sugru, the British Blu-Tack firm that was sold at a knockdown price in 2017, with 4,700 shareholders losing 90% of their money. Or online estate agent eMoov, which crashed into administration in 2018 a few months after raising £1.8m on Crowdcube from 1000 investors.

Even crowdfunding platforms admit only a minority of campaigns succeed, with studies suggesting roughly 60% of companies that raise early-stage funds will fail within five years. That number is only likely to rise in years to come as we emerge from the economic wreckage of Covid-19.

If crowdfunding does take your fancy, here's how to do it smartly. Only allocate a small percentage of your money in any one year to it – no more than 5% – and try to spread your money across multiple campaigns in the hope one or two might beat the odds. Expect to wait five to seven years at least, as you'll probably only capture your gains if the business gets sold or goes public.

Returns on crowdfunding ain't copper-bottomed. The shares you acquire may not rise in value, you may not receive any dividend or share of the profits, and it may also be hard to sell your shares, as they are not listed on any exchange. There may only be a yearly or half-yearly dealing opportunity – in other words, no easy way out.

Above all, read the goddam prospectus for any investment you are pondering! The prospectus should tell you:

- How much the business wants to raise.
- How much it has raised so far.
- The share in the business offered.
- What the money will be specifically used for.

- How long the pitch is open.
- How many people have invested.
- What you will receive in return.

Above all, the information provided must be detailed and plausible: beware a mega-high valuation and airy-fairy waffle.

Innovative Finance ISA: the alt-finance vehicle

If you decide to dabble in P2P or crowdfunding, you can do so through an Innovative Finance ISA. This is part of your £20,000 ISA allowance you get every tax year and means any and all returns you make will be tax free.

Minibonds, massive risks

EXAMPLE 872 OF how the financial world loves to confuse ordinary folks: the use of 'bonds' in so many contexts to mean so many things. We've already looked at savings bonds, government bonds and corporate bonds, but you can also get **minibonds**, which are basically a form of high-risk corporate debt.

You lend your cash to a company in return for a seemingly superior fixed interest rate (say, 8%) and supposedly get your money back at the end of the term. Provided the outfit isn't a scam or doesn't go bust, of course!

Minibonds are similar to P2P in offering flashy returns and, as with crowdfunding, sometimes throw gimmicks into the mix to drum up interest. More than 1,000 people bought £5.8m worth of minibonds issued by Chilango, a restaurant group, which promised a free burrito a week for everyone who paid in more than £10,000. But when Chilango went into administration, these investments became nigh-on worthless. Hope the burritos were worth it…

Seriously though, I don't blame investors for failing to spot the risks: these minibonds can be marketed in a deeply misleading way. Take London Capital & Finance, which went bust in January 2019 and is mired in legal challenges over allegations of fraud. Many investors came across its minibonds after seeing paid-for adverts on Google when they searched for terms like 'best savings accounts'. The marketing boasted of much higher fixed rates compared to savings and authorisation from the FCA.

Say no to clickbait investing

The truth was that the minibonds weren't regulated, only the company offering them, leaving 12,000 investors with losses totalling £236m. The FCA has now banned the marketing of minibonds to so-called 'ordinary' savers, though a quick search of Google at time of writing STILL shows companies marketing investments to people searching for savings bonds (shaking my head…).

Until the internet giants get their act together, you've got no choice but to ignore paid-for financial ads on Google or social media. Following clickbait is no way to invest, nor is being led by cheap beer 'n' burritos, much as I *heart* both.

So now we've covered the whole gamut of assets – the good, the bad and the silly – you are at the point where you can start to make informed and intelligent investing decisions.

High five! I knew you could do it! Now let's firm up your strategy.

CHAPTER 20

Sussing out your strategy!

IT'S DECISION TIME! You've learned about all the main asset classes, as well as the various types of apps and platforms you can use to start your investing journey.

This chapter now covers what you'll need to bear in mind as you create your investing strategy.

Lots of concepts, terms and topics I bring up here should already ring a bell, as many of them have been sprinkled throughout the book so far. But it's worth having a big ol' recap and bringing the key stuff all together in one place, so that by the time you head into my bonus chapter, you should be fairly fluent in the language of investing.

As you start putting your strategy together, you'll also have to choose what kind of tech you want to use to execute it. That's why I recommend going back and having another look at chapters 12–15, now you understand how all the options highlighted in that part of the book fit into the overall landscape and which ones might be best for your needs, circumstances and wishes.

There are no definitively right or wrong answers. And you may choose to use a combination (as I have done). But if you go through the considerations I outline in this chapter, that should make your decisions smarter *and* easier.

So let's crack on!

How do you approach risk?

RISK IS A fact of life and you'll have your own attitude to it.

You may be the kind of person who likes to be adventurous, try new things and chase thrills. Think extreme sports and holidaying in North Korea.

Or you might be the kind of person who wants to protect what you've got, craves creature comforts, and enjoys the simple things in life. Think early nights and Michael Bublé.

Most of us fall somewhere in between. Investing is also about striking the right balance. We can get much more out of life and move forward by taking calculated risks: fortune does favour the brave. But it doesn't favour the reckless or those chasing highs in crazy places.

When it comes to money, there are no risk-free choices. While putting cash in the bank is the safest thing you can do, there is actually such a thing as "reckless conservatism"[126] where we lose money in real terms as inflation erodes our cash (see chapter 1). Or where we invest our pension in assets that are too cautious, leaving us with a big shortfall in our retirement income (see chapter 7).

Whatever your attitude to risk, you will always need to take basic precautions, like diversifying your portfolio across different assets and markets. That involves comparing the risks and rewards offered by different asset classes.

So, welcome to the Risk Spectrum! At the safest end of the spectrum are the assets that have offered the lower historic investment returns, notably cash.

As you move up the risk spectrum, there are assets with higher historic returns but they also involve more risk, so you need to hold onto these investments for longer to increase the chances of earning a positive return. Shares are the prime example.

There are also risk scales within asset classes themselves, though the categories are more fluid and can change over time.

For instance, if we take equities as an example, so-called **blue chips** (i.e. large, well-established companies) are *traditionally* regarded as being safer investments as they should have the resources to withstand an economic downturn.

But just because a company is large doesn't mean it's invincible. British Airways is in the FTSE 100, but it was battered by unprecedented travel restrictions during Covid-19. And profits from large oil companies and banks may be threatened by future moves towards a greener economy and tougher financial regulations. Smaller and newer firms, meanwhile, may be theoretically riskier investments, but it very much depends on the sector they are in and what kind of company they are.

Also, you need to accept that if you're naturally more cautious, you're never going to be comfortable with an ultra-aggressive investment portfolio where the value of your investments could rise and fall a lot over time. If you are cautious, make peace with the fact that your returns will most likely lag those of more gung-ho investors. Therein lies the trade-off between risk and reward!

Be honest with yourself and don't act tough for its own sake. Only do what's right for you.

How much time and energy are you prepared to invest in... investing?

SOME PEOPLE HAVE the capacity and curiosity about investing stuff to manage their portfolio in a hands-on way. These investors gravitate towards DIY platforms and trading apps, investing in individual companies and assets.

Other people are time-poor and less confident in their ability to beat expert fund managers or the performance of overall stock indices, like the FTSE. They lean on robo and real-life advisers, active and passive funds, and/or ETFs. These options aren't automatically more cautious: you can still choose more adventurous versions of them all.

Remember, contrary to what some online investing nerds would have you believe, this isn't a competition. You're not a better, smarter person just because you manage all your own investments. There is nothing wrong with seeking some help, even – or perhaps especially – if you're a more self-assured character who thinks, "yea, I've got this!"

All investors, from beginners up to George Soros, need to be aware of what they don't know. Only then can they work out how to become more enlightened and look for ways to manage their risks.

Stocks and shares ISA: is it worth your while?

I talked about the ISA family, and particularly the LISA, in part 1. But we didn't discuss the stocks and shares ISA.

The conventional advice has always been to treat the stocks and shares ISA as your first port of call when you start investing, because of its tax-free status. In truth, you would have to currently be making £12,000 in profits a year and/or earning dividends worth more than £2000 to be better off with an ISA compared to a general investment account.

Obviously, these tax allowances may be tweaked in the future, but it may be worth checking if a platform charges extra for running an ISA, which you may not actually need. The industry argues that one day, you will have a huge portfolio where the tax breaks will come into their own. I suppose a girl can dream!

Will you go active or passive?

I HAVE ALREADY discussed the active vs passive face-off in chapter 12 and you may be starting to decide which side you favour.

The passive path

Investors who aren't convinced that human fund managers can consistently **beat the index** – i.e. do better than the aggregate performance of companies in a particular market – might go for those **exchange traded funds** I mentioned in chapter 12.

If you go down that road, you need to assess which indices may perform best in the coming years and choose a decent collection of ETFs: being invested in one or two, just because they seem to cover lots of companies or a wide geographic footprint, won't offer you enough diversification.

You also need to be aware of the difference between the buy price and sell price of an ETF, i.e. the **spread**. The smaller the spread, the smaller the cost that will be deducted from your return when you come to sell.

Alternatively, another passive path is to go direct to Vanguard's platform and look at its five LifeStrategy funds. These are 'one-stop shop' portfolios made up of multiple tracker funds. Each of them varies the split between equities and bonds, ranging from the most cautious having 80% in bonds and 20% in equities, right up to the highest risk being invested 100% in equities. The ongoing charge is a respectable 0.22% a year.

Going global

A classic beginner choice is a **global** fund, which is one single fund that holds shares in companies all over the world. It spreads risk by investing across different economies.

The MSCI World Index, which measures the value of the bigger companies in 23 developed economies, is dominated by the US market, which accounts for around two-thirds of the index. The UK had (as of June 2020) a share of under 5%, Japan 8%, and the four biggest European markets 11%.[127]

A global fund, especially if it is an index tracker, will be spread in a similar way. If you invest in this fund, you are buying shares in the overall world economy.

If you'd like a more fine-tuned approach, you could curate a portfolio of individual funds invested in different regions around the world. One fund might invest in the UK, another in Europe, a third in Japan, and a fourth in the US.

Or you could pick one fund investing globally and add funds aimed at Asia, or specifically China, or funds investing in **emerging markets**. Emerging markets are historically low-income countries that are fast becoming modern, industrialised economies, like Russia, Brazil and India. They have huge promise but may also hit some political and economic turbulence along the way, so they are riskier than **developed markets** like the US, Europe and the UK.

Let's get active

But maybe you don't want to give up on active fund managers just yet. Indeed, you could try having your cake and eating it by having some core tracker funds, but also backing an active fund or two, run by managers with an impressive track record. This is a particularly smart idea in areas that need a more specialist eye on them, such as smaller companies and more niche markets. Indeed, the consensus is that active funds rarely beat trackers in large markets heavily picked over by investors, but can have the edge in sectors off the beaten track.

Funds report their value every day, and they measure their performance against a **benchmark**. A fund investing in the UK will probably have the benchmark of the FTSE All-Share index covering every share listed on the main market of the London Stock Exchange. A global fund will measure itself against a global index like the MSCI.

Performance is usually recorded over one, three and five years. An active fund worth a look will have 'beaten its benchmark' over all those time periods. You'll want to find funds which have hit this bullseye consistently.

We can't forget that past performance is no guide to the future. But actually, it's about the only guide there is. Just don't stake ALL your financial hopes and dreams on it, 'kay?

Theme dream

For part of your portfolio, you might want to think about going **thematic**, finding active funds or ETFs which track companies in future-focused areas like robotics, green energy and cyber-security. And this is the moment to decide whether you want to go full-blown ESG or not. Remember, in chapter 11, we found that you don't necessarily have to decide between performance and principles.

In fact, ESG funds outperformed their non-ESG competitors in 2020, across both global and UK equity markets,[128] as investors ploughed four times as much cash into ESG as they did in 2019.[129] Recent research has shown that funds badged as ethical performed better than their less scrupulous counterparts and only slightly behind globally. Don't forget that 'ethical' funds may not always be what they seem and ESG fund management can be more expensive, as it requires investment managers and their analysts to conduct more research. Investors in funds have to pay for this research through fund management fees. Passive ESG funds are cheaper, but as we saw in chapter 11, even active investors differ in their interpretations of what is ethical, so outsourcing that knotty process to a robot may not exactly get you the results you desire.

Average ten-year return: ESG vs non-ESG

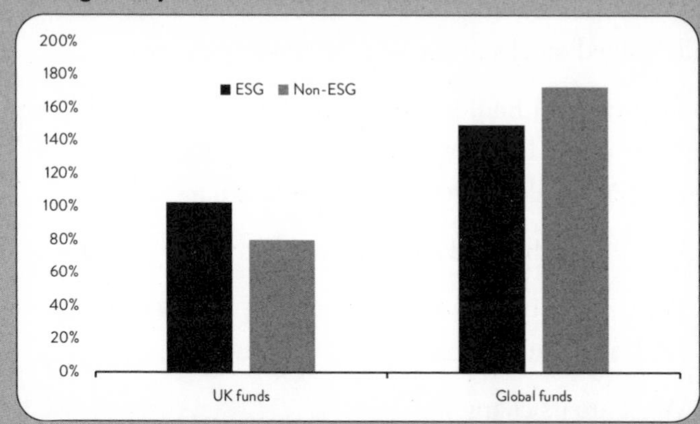

Source: AJ Bell

Which investment styles will you back?

KNOWING WHAT FUNDS do matters. One of the most popular UK funds, called Lindsell Train, was ranked 151 out of 160 funds in 2008. So clearly one to avoid like the plague, right? But market conditions changed, and 12 years later it was the second-best fund out of 182 in the list.

One reason for this is that funds have different **styles** or strategies. For instance, some will do better when the economy is booming because they invest in companies that benefit from confident consumers making it rain. These are called **cyclical** stocks because they are more sensitive to the inevitable economic cycle of boom and bust. If everything slows down, those companies' profits will slide, their share prices will sag, and the funds investing in them will not perform as well. Other funds will aim to be more **defensive**, prospering when times are tougher.

Another divide is between funds aimed at **growth** – investing in fast-growing companies – those aimed at **income**, i.e. investing in companies which pay higher dividends (see chapter 18), and those aimed at **value**, where fund managers will target 'undervalued' stocks in the hope their day will come.

So how can you find out what a fund is all about? Well, every fund has a Key Investor Information Document (KIID). It's a two-pager. It will answer three important questions:

1. What does the fund aim to do and how does it do this?
2. What is its 'risk profile' on a scale of 1 (very cautious) to 7 (very adventurous)?
3. What are its charges?

You should also be able to dig a bit deeper if you want to. Funds have factsheets which show their top ten investments. And what about the manager? Have they been there forever, or did they take over quite recently?

Longevity can be good sign. Some eight of the ten longest-serving managers of funds have beaten the benchmark of their fund during their tenure, while nine out of ten veteran investment trust managers have done so over the long term.[130] But veteran managers can lose their touch, so don't be too overawed by a stunning track record.

In 2019, the spectacular fall of Neil Woodford, the so-called rock star of active fund management, shocked the investment world. After years of thrashing the index while at a major investment house (Invesco), Woodford set up his own firm and, high on his success, junked his tried-and-tested formula to chase sexy, high-risk investments (like biotech start-ups).

Yet this racy portfolio was sold to Mom 'n' Pop, as they say over the pond, as a mass-market equity income fund. After a series of individual stock disasters and increasingly concerned media reports, investors fled the fund, causing it to be gated and eventually wound up, losing existing investors up to 43% of their money. Want to know more? I recommend *When the Fund Stops*, all about this scandal, by David Ricketts.

How will you get your investing info and recommendations?

IF YOU DON'T use a human financial adviser or robo-adviser, you'll have to get up to speed all on your own. Funds get written about in the financial media or on investor websites and are analysed in forensic detail on sites like Morningstar. But it's a gigantic investment galaxy which can be overwhelming for first-time investors.

Bigger platforms offer suggestions and guidance, in the form of 'lists', but I refer you to chapter 12 on why you should perhaps take these with a large pinch of salt. Sometimes, they can offer useful ideas. What they don't offer is a quality Kitemark you can rely on. You need to go à la carte with your fund choices, rather than fixate on the set menu.

Otherwise, I recommend reading the Money sections of national newspapers – which is how I learned most of the basics of personal finance and investing – plus checking out my four more specialist resources below.

Four money bibles that have got your back

Finimize (finimize.com)

Aimed at a new generation of investors, Finimize sends subscribers daily email updates on markets, peppered with emojis, pun-tastic headlines and thought-provoking quotes. Basic emails with ads are free but you can upgrade at £8.99 a month to receive premium insights, more in-depth information packs and access to VIP events with high-quality speakers.

Moneyweek (moneyweek.com)

Get ultra-informed about everything happening in the world of money, from macro-economics to personal finance. Authoritative but accessible: the perfect combo. A digital subscription costs £24.69, though there is usually an offer to receive several issues for free.

Financial Times (ft.com)

I couldn't ignore the FT, could I? You can geek out with its Companies & Markets and FTFM (fund management) coverage, but beginners can start on the nursery slopes of the outstanding Money section and *FT* Money Clinic podcast. A digital subscription is on the pricier side at £33 per month, but think of it as being cheaper than most gym memberships and a worthwhile investment in its own right.

Boring Money (boringmoney.co.uk)

This is one of the few free consumer-facing sites that is accurate, expert-led AND down to earth when it comes to investing. It goes to a lot of trouble to assess various investing options and thoughtfully answer readers' questions.

In addition, there are several online tools springing up to help newbie stock pickers make sense of companies' investment potential, such as Genuine Impact and Simply Wall St. But while these offer useful, jargon-free data about companies, they don't and can't make your investing decisions for you. Ultimately, the buck stops with you, kiddo!

Don't get psyched out

PHEW! WE HAVE almost reached the end. By now, you should have a pretty good idea of how you'll start your investing journey, what technology you might use, what you should think about when drawing up your investing strategy, and what you should rule out or treat with kid gloves.

But talking and reading about this stuff is not the same as *doing* it. And you can have the best investing plan in the world on paper, only to chuck it out the window and let your primal desires, fear and greed take over as soon as real money is at stake.

If that happens, you can kiss your goals and dreams goodbye, because there can be no surer way to lose money than to let your amygdala – the small almond-shaped collection of cells in your brain that trigger emotional responses – run the show.

A myth about investing is that it is a dry and purely technical business, when actually it's incredibly emotional. How can it not be, when we're tying up our precious money in the changing fates and fortunes of the stock market?

Being a successful investor is as much about understanding how your brain is liable to react in real, difficult situations and learning to override certain instincts as it is about grasping the numbers. This isn't about whipping ourselves over our weaknesses or waging psychological warfare on our own brains, but acknowledging that we're only human, and accepting our natural responses need to be actively countered with a cool, rational mindset and some firm rules.

I can't get inside your head. But I can let you get inside mine, and help you learn from my successes and mistakes out in the field. It's time to let you peek inside my investing diary… eek!

BONUS CHAPTER

My 2020 investing diary

SO, THERE I was in early 2020, wrapping up this book, planning a wee staycation to recharge my batteries and keeping half an eye on my own little portfolio of investments, which were bobbing along nicely.

I had already built up a decent portfolio in my LISA – which I was managing myself through an investment platform – to help fund my retirement, as I'm self-employed and already on the property ladder. But I had recently decided I needed to start a private pension through a robo-adviser to make sure I could contribute more towards my retirement as my earnings grew. I was also using some of my ISA allowance to fund a stocks and shares ISA over the medium term.

I had started investing in the 2010s, when the stock markets seemed to be absolutely smashing it. What could go wrong?

A viral pandemic, that's what!

The c-word came along and turned all our lives upside down. All our social, cultural, and personal plans went out the window. But Houston, we had an even bigger problem. The stock market was about to hit its biggest bout of turbulence since 2008, when financial journalism and investing was a mere twinkle in my eye.

To use a technical investing phrase, shit was about to get real. So, when the chips were down and I had some real money in the markets, how would I actually respond?

Well, you can find out for yourself. I'm opening up my investing diary* so that you can understand what it's really like to invest in a downturn. At the end, I'll share the main lessons I've learned and leave you with my eight golden rules.

24 February

Monday. Coronavirus has reached a 'tipping point', say the medical boffins. Blimey. This lurgy could be a lot worse than I initially thought.

The FTSE 100 is down 261 points or 3.5%, while the US stock market is down more than 2%. Gold, that classic safe haven in troubled times, is up 2%. Trouble's brewing. Still, the book's going well, and I've found this lovely little yoga retreat in Devon. I'll get booking for early April!

27 February

Thursday. FTSE down 3.2% today. Everyone else must know something I don't?! This is the first time I can remember that the FTSE has kept falling over a whole week. Surely this is as bad as it gets?! At least it's nearly the weekend…

* Okay, I admit this isn't the word-for-word diary I kept at the time and I have taken some artistic licence, inspired by Bridget Jones, to bring these issues to life. But the events described are factual, and what I say about my investing situation, actions, and feelings during this period is v true.

28 February

Friday. FTSE down 4.5% as the virus is starting to spread. Luckily, the market's closed tomorrow, otherwise I might start listening to that little voice in my head telling me to sell up. Must. Not. Listen!

6 March

Yippee! The markets bounced back over the past three days after interest rates were cut in the US. Let me just check my… oh. Markets are down 3.5% today, wiping out all the gains from that little false rally. Now I know what they mean by a 'dead cat bounce'. RIP Fluffy, it was nice while it lasted.

9 March

Okay. Now I'm officially triggered. The price of oil plummeted by 20% and the US market was suspended at the start of trading, so it didn't implode altogether. The FTSE is down a whopping 7.7%. I didn't think that was even possible! Meanwhile, Italy put 16 million people in quarantine yesterday.

I'm not even going to *look* at my portfolios, unless I want a good cry. I *know* I shouldn't rush into any emotional decisions. Nothing has fundamentally changed since I started investing. My stocks and shares ISA was doing perfectly well before, and it'll do perfectly well again. And my LISA and pensions are for my retirement, for Pete's sake! Just got to sit tight and wait.

But it's so hard when you feel something's broke and you just want to fix it. It's a primal human instinct, the urge to protect what we've got. Not that cavemen were fretting over the share price of Furs 'R' Us, but still… perhaps if I sell my falling assets,

I'll start to feel better. What harm can it do? Then I could buy it all back when it gets really cheap.

But when the hell will THAT be? I think I see the problem. As the investing boffins say, "the bell doesn't ring at the bottom" (or the top) – or to bring it up to date, I shouldn't expect a WhatsApp 'ding!' when it's time to buy back in. So, I'm telling my inner cavewoman to shut up, not least because she's also telling me that I should be stockpiling loo roll.

12 March

Woah. It's a good job I bought more toilet paper. The FTSE 100 has crashed by 10.9%, its second-biggest daily fall in history. President Trump has banned air travel, the US market is down 7%, and it's the worst day ever for European markets.

The US Federal Reserve is going to print some money and throw it at the crisis. Who knows if it will work?! Somehow, I don't think I'll be doing downward dogs in Devon anytime soon, and it's clear I'll have to make some changes to my book. Make mine an extra-strong G 'n'T…

23 March

I can't believe what's happening. The Prime Minister told the nation tonight that everyone must stay at home except for essential reasons. The poor old FTSE 100 is down 234 points today and now it's below not 6000 but 5000. That means it's down by almost a third in four weeks. Will it ever go back up?

I can't help feeling I should have bailed out when it all started… I know I've done the right thing but that's not much consolation right now. I'm off to bake some banana bread and figure out how the hell Zoom works.

25 March

Yeesh, the news is bleak ATM. But hey! At least the FTSE is getting its mojo back. It was up 9% yesterday, one of its best days ever, and another 4.5% today. The US is passing a $2 trillion coronavirus stimulus bill, and the chancellor is digging deep with a furlough scheme to pay people's wages in shutdown sectors. Perhaps the economic hit won't be as bad as it could have been…

27 March

Right, maybe it's time for me to actually do something with my investments… no no, not sell them all, obvs! But in my LISA I'm selling one holding at a profit, and I'm ploughing that, plus some uninvested cash, into four investment trusts that I already hold. Yes, I'm following the advice of none other than Warren Buffett, the legendary US investor. He's not a billionaire and so-called Sage of Omaha, where he hails from, for nowt.

He says that when there's a crash, you should buy more of what you already have. Seriously. Because when the price goes up again (fingers crossed) you will break even and then make a profit at a much lower level than before. Ahhh! That makes sense. I'll have to wait a while to see how it works, but then this is a LISA so I've got oodles of time. 27 years to be precise! As for my pension, I've just got to trust that the guys looking after it are taking some sensible decisions to help protect my money, but ultimately, this blip shouldn't affect it too much in the long run.

29 April

Woohoo! There's been a successful vaccine trial and signs that lockdowns may be eased. Another five weeks on from the ghastly month of March and the FTSE 100 is back above 6000. Who would have believed it?

In my stocks and shares ISA, I've sold two ETFs and an investment trust that had all made a little money and recycled it into two trusts I already hold which look bombed out. I'm prepared to be a bit more active in my ISA as it's not intended as a super long-term savings home. But I know I must control the urge to trade too much as the costs do add up.

20 May

Wowsers, I am amazed at how quickly markets have rebounded. I'm reading about an investing boom among young people and I can't say I'm surprised. Sure, lockdowns are easing, but trillions have also been pumped into the markets… loads of people thought sky-high US tech stocks like Amazon would finally go into reverse due to the crisis, but nope. They just keep on climbing.

Maybe I should buy in? I don't want to miss out. A new tax year began in April, so I have a new ISA allowance and I may just open an account with Freetrade, just to see what it's like…

19 June

I stumble across some alternative investing forums, where the crypto community is talking about how the smart money is increasingly wrapped up in Bitcoin. I wonder if now's the time to switch things up, if this is indeed what all the clever clogs are doing.

As fate would have it, I later read about the financial decisions of someone who is widely considered to be a genius. In 1720, Sir Isaac Newton held a £7000 stake (then worth £3.5m) in the South Sea Company and sold it for a 100% profit, banking the equivalent of £7m. He wrote that the price had been inflated by people's "madness". But when the price climbed even higher, he was tortured by the Big R of regret when he missed out on even bigger gains.

Swayed by the hysteria of the ever-rising price, he ploughed an enormous sum – £20,000 or about £10m today – back into the South Sea Company. You guessed it – he lost it all. Maybe that apple hit his bonce a bit too hard. I think I'll steer clear of Bitcoin, thankyouverymuch.

4 July

Yay, pubs and restaurants are open! And so is my Freetrade ISA! It was so easy – open within five minutes. Oooh I do like their app, they have little snapshots of companies' performance showing whether they're up or down… I could get used to this. I dip my toes in the water with some futuristic ETFs after reading an article on the financial website Citywire by David Stevenson that discussed promising future trends, like gaming, water technologies, global robotics and biotech.[131]

I also grab some investment trusts spread across different regions and sectors that are on decent discounts, and a few shares that are in the doldrums but are fundamentally well-run companies that are sure to come back. Like Greggs. Who doesn't like Greggs?

7 July

I am obsessed. This app is addictive. I keep checking my ISA, even when markets are closed. It's up 3%! Then it's down 2%! Then it's up 10%! I see their most popular stocks on the home screen and I get raging FOMO. Why didn't I buy Tesla? Sure, I know CEO Elon Musk is a bit weird, and there's a huge debate around whether Tesla shares are unshakeable or a bloated bubble.

Still, it's hard not to feel like a total mug for having a broad, diverse portfolio when others are going all in on US tech, and so far, winning big. Wahhh. I decide I need to forget about my investments and enjoy the sunshine – and maybe freedom? – while it lasts.

9 July

I'm in recovery. My loved ones staged an intervention. I have stopped checking my new ISA every five seconds. I've got it down to once a day, but I know that's still too often. I peruse the *FT* with a strong cup of tea and read some good advice that helps me to *Step Away from the Phone*.

In the *FT*, Madison Darbyshire writes that the "more connected you are to the daily, or hourly, market swings, the more you will be focused on the short-term, and the more likely you are to make impulsive choices".[132] This is exacerbated in times of crisis, but often, doing nothing is the best course of action.

Hmm. Maybe I shouldn't have sold any of my successful holdings earlier this year, as they'd be up even more by now. But then again, what's the point in having regrets or wishing you'd made even more money? That's just me being a greedy guts.

17 August

I've been a good girl and left my portfolios untouched. The FTSE is still plodding along around 6000. Seems like that stomach-churning fall in March really was the worst of it. Or was it?

Everyone's worried about a second wave of the virus, not to mention massive unemployment and recession if the chancellor turns off the financial taps. I'd better strap in for some more volatility!

28 August

I can't resist any longer. I want a piece of the tech action, so I buy Apple's shares when they split 4-to-1. Companies do this when they want to lower their share prices, allowing smaller investors (like me!) to buy in, without reducing their value. Apple's shares have been rocketing for some time so surely it's a good decision…?

9 September

What was I thinking?! There's been a huge sell-off in tech shares these past three days, and guess which company has fallen the most? Apple, dropping 6.7% today. Turns out buying in *after* a share split may not be such a smart move. It looks like we have hit the peak of Apple mania. The only consolation is that my stake is tiny.

It doesn't help that only a handful of my investments – mainly investment trusts – are doing okay, with the rest of my portfolio taking an absolute bath. With a new lockdown on the horizon, maybe buying Greggs wasn't such a good idea either.

9 November

HALLELUJAH! The news that Pfizer's Covid-19 vaccine may be 90% effective has made the stock markets delirious.

It's super early days, but it looks like life will return to normal at some point. Even my shares in Greggs are in the black, but I'm very glad I had my investment trusts, with their diversification and smart allocation, to outweigh some of my iffier stock picks.

My investing comfort zone is global and UK investment trusts/ETFs, and this is the first year I have branched out into picking individual shares and more thematic ETFs. While I've learned an awful lot, I have a long way to go in establishing a more rigorous process for future decision-making. That said, I feel I'm reaching towards a strategy that could suit me and my needs: a portfolio invested in cheap, unloved companies, solid blue-chip stocks, futuristic sectors and the burgeoning green revolution might come good in the end.

And with the vaccine on the way, perhaps I will finally get to do my sun salutations in a beautiful corner of England one day. Namaste!

My eight golden rules

SO WHAT DID I learn from the crazy year that was 2020? Apart from remembering to unmute myself on Zoom, here are the main takeaways.

1. Diversify

Boy was I glad that I wasn't over-invested in one area, even Big Tech. That doesn't mean the FAANGs (and Tesla) won't continue to grow and perform well in the future, and it would be worth having some exposure to the big beasts dominating the US stock market (and our lives). But history suggests rolling your investments across different regions, sectors and styles will pay off. It was also good to be invested in a range of ETFs and investment trusts alongside (or instead of) some daredevil share picks. This all helps to achieve more diversification.

2. In the main, invest for the long term

This is not to say that you can't sell shares along the way to top up your short-term funds. Don't have any regrets if prices keep rising after you sell up: if you make a decent profit, be #thankful. But often, it may be better to stick around and see what happens in the long run. I can't judge those trades in my ISA based on a few weeks or months – I'll only know in years to come if they've paid off.

3. Drip-feed your money

Have a decent lump sum to invest? Lucky you! But I recommend parcelling it up into 12 pieces and feeding in one piece a month for a year. It's less risky to invest small amounts regularly rather than chucking a big sum in one go. That way, if you do happen to pick the worst possible time, you'll escape the worst result – possibly halving your potential loss.[133]

4. Get your geek on

You need to have a solid, fact-based rationale for the investments you pick. That's only possible by getting informed and properly reading up on any investments you're pondering.

I'm not proposing that you become an investing dweeb glued to the markets every day. I have what I call an 'information circuit' of websites, newspapers, podcasts, magazines, and social feeds that I trust to give me an overview of what's going on. I typically check them out once a week – sometimes more frequently in unusual periods like 2020, when opportunities to buy cheaply may present themselves.

If you're mulling over an investment, try to really understand what its valuation is based on, how it compares with competitors or other regions/sectors, and how it might *realistically* be affected by external events. It's easy to persuade yourself that all news will be good news for an investment that takes your fancy, but you have to be dispassionate.

5. Don't follow the crowd

Buying something simply because everyone else, even your Aunty Maureen, is buying it is plain silly. Often, it's not because they know something you don't. In fact, they may not know something that you do: namely, that it's far better to pick a strategy suitable for the long term and stick with it, save for a few tweaks here and there. However smart someone seems, that doesn't mean they'll make good investing decisions. Remember Isaac Newton: great at grasping gravity, awful at conserving his wealth!

6. Trade less, not more

Feeling the urge to tinker with your portfolio? Unless you've really thought through a new investing decision, or perhaps are buying more of what you have in falling markets or capturing some decent profits, resist it. Do some judo, pottery, Tinder swiping, whatever floats your boat, until the moment passes.

7. Be cool!

If you can keep your head when all about you are losing theirs… the upsides of the stock markets will be yours, to very loosely paraphrase Rudyard Kipling.

8. If it sounds too good to be true...

Well, you know the answer to this by now, don't you? Consistently high returns cannot be guaranteed because investing is inherently uncertain. Nobody, including me, can tell you what's going to happen.

Some people and companies will tell you what you want to hear, particularly in a frightening, messy and uncertain year like 2020. They'll pretend that there is an easy, smooth route away from the unpredictable, rocky nature of investing. But the truth is that there is no way to bypass the investing rollercoaster: you've just got to hop on, stay strapped in, and try to enjoy the ride.

Signing off

I HOPE YOU have enjoyed and learned as much reading *Own It!* as I have writing it. This book has been a labour of love, born out of my conviction that young people have an incredible opportunity to really own their financial futures post-Covid, but need a trustworthy, relatable friend to guide them through the maze that is modern investing.

I have tried to make this book as comprehensive as possible, but with something as vast as investing, I have not been able to cover everything. But I hope this book has inspired you to get started and laid down the groundwork for your investing journey. It's up to you what path you take.

The information contained in this book is correct and up to date as of late 2020, but may change following publication, so please do double check things.

Please note that I am not a qualified financial adviser. This book should be interpreted as general guidance only. It's important to seek regulated and independent financial advice if you want specific recommendations based on your personal situation.

If you have any further questions relating to your circumstances, you can search for a qualified adviser in your area using the Chartered Institute for Securities & Investment's Wayfinder database at financialplanning.org.uk/wayfinder/find-planner or the Personal Finance Society's database at thepfs.org/yourmoney/find-an-adviser.

Finally, please let me know how you plan to own it! You can contact me through my website – youngmoneyblog.co.uk – and spread the joys of owning it with your friends and followers. Share what you've learned and/or what you'll do next on social media using the hashtag #ownit (and tag me if you can!).

All that's left for me to say is good luck. Let's go and own it!

Thanks

FIRSTLY, I WANT to thank the various agents and publishers who rejected this book at first glance by wrongly identifying it as too similar to others in the market. Otherwise, I would never have found Harriman House, the most supportive, knowledgeable, professional, and lovely bunch of people I could ever hope to work with. No other publisher would have done such an incredible job with *Own It!* – it was a match made in heaven and I will always be grateful to John Stepek, the executive editor of *MoneyWeek*, for introducing us.

A huge thank you to my main man Craig Pearce for his never-ending patience, encouragement, constructive suggestions and diligent editing, which have enhanced this book no end. I also want to thank Emma Tinker for her all-important millennial perspective; Christopher Parker and the design team for making this book look so bad-ass; and Lucy Scott for doing such a brilliant job so far on getting *Own It!* out there. Thanks must also go to Ian Pringle, who virtually held my hand as I undertook the mighty process of narrating the audiobook for *Own It!* from my living room in lockdown – he was a star.

I am fortunate to have had many mentors and supporters since I embarked on this career. They have given me so many opportunities to learn and succeed. These include individuals like *FT* Adviser editor Simoney Kyriakou and Margaret Taylor, formerly of the *Herald*; Alex Lewis, Jim Booth and Fiona Bruce at the BBC; Mark Bridge and Mark Atherton at the *Times*, and its former money editor, Anne Ashworth; James Coney and Becky Barrow at the *Sunday Times*; Baroness Altman; Holly Mackay at Boring Money; Kevin Carr; Daniel Godfrey; Merryn Somerset Webb at *MoneyWeek*; Tony Langham and Clare Parsons at Lansons; and organisations like the Pensions and Lifetime Savings Association, the Association of Financial Mutuals, Baillie Gifford, the Scottish Investment Trust, Nucleus and my former publisher, Hardie Grant. There are many more people and organisations which have supported me and Young Money along the way: you know who are, thank you.

Special thanks is reserved for the *FT*'s Consumer (and former Money) editor Claer Barrett, who has been my kindest, most steadfast champion in recent years; IPSE (the Association for Independent Professionals and the Self-Employed), for providing crucial funding and credibility for Young Money; and JLA, my speaking agency.

Last but not least, I want to thank my semi-retired dad, Simon Bain, former personal finance editor at the *Herald*; my mum, Norma; and my brother, Matt. Together they provided vast amounts of intellectual, practical, emotional and caffeinated help while I conceived and wrote this book. Countless hours were spent with them thrashing out whether *Own It!* was a good idea, how best to execute it and how to overcome the obstacles along the way.

In particular, this book would never have happened without Simon, who was always there for me from inception to completion, either providing hands-on research, experience and wisdom, or helping me manage the day-to-day running of Young Money. Words can't fully express my gratitude, but hopefully the result is a book that he, and all my wonderful family, can be proud of.

Endnotes

1 Jonathan Cribb and Paul Johnson, '10 years on – have we recovered from the financial crisis?', IFS (12 September 2018).

2 Sarah O'Connor, 'Graduate data reveal England's lost and indebted generation', *Financial Times* (18 November 2013).

3 'The graduate employment gap: expectations versus reality', CIPD (16 November 2017).

4 Stephen Clarke, 'Growing Pains', Resolution Foundation (May 2019).

5 Rob Merrick, 'Housebuilding figures under Conservatives lowest since the Second World War', *Independent* (1 January 2019).

6 'A New Generational Contract: The final report of the Intergenerational Commission', Resolution Foundation (8 May 2018); and Michael Savage, 'Millennial housing crisis engulfs Britain', *Guardian* (28 April 2018).

7 'Family spending in the UK: April 2017 to March 2018', ONS (24 January 2019).

8 George Bangham, 'Game of Homes: The rise of multiple property ownership in Great Britain', Resolution Foundation (15 June 2019).

9 Dharshini David, 'Was the millennial dream killed by QE?' BBC (8 March 2019).

10 'Bank of mum and dad "one of UK's biggest mortgage lenders"', BBC (27 August 2019).

11 'A New Generational Contract', Resolution Foundation.

12 'A New Generational Contract', Resolution Foundation.

13 'Discover more about intergenerational wealth transfers', Kings Court Trust.

14 'Millennials expect to inherit £1.2 trillion in the next 30 years', Sanlam (29 June 2018).

15 Pascale Bourquin, Robert Joyce and David Sturrock, 'Inherited wealth on course to be a much more important determinant of lifetime resources for today's young than it was for previous generations', IFS (22 July 2020).

16 Resolution Foundation.

17 Resolution Foundation.

18 Gideon Skinner, 'Financial impact of Covid-19 already being felt by Britons, especially younger generations', Ipsos MORI (7 April 2020).

19 'Coronavirus: Young people on benefits double in lockdown', BBC (20 July 2020).

20 *Merriam-Webster*.

21 *Cambridge Dictionary*.

22 Barclays Equity Gilt Study 2019.

23 'Cash Beat Shares From 1995 To 2015', Paul Lewis Money (14 June 2016).

24 'Intergenerational Differences', FCA Discussion Paper (May 2019).

25 Callum Cliffe, 'What is a stock market correction and how can you trade one?', IG.com (25 March 2020).

26 Ian Cowie, 'Two world wars and a depression, and still shares emerge victorious', *Sunday Times* (14 April 2019).

27 Stuart Fieldhouse, 'Millennials charging into stocks and shares ISAs says Scottish Friendly', The Armchair Trader (22 July 2020).

28 Martin Lewis, 'Student Loans Mythbusting', MoneySavingExpert.com.

29 'How to get credit for the first time', the Money Advice Service.

30 Abdulkader Mostafa and Colin Jones, 'Rent or buy: does the British obsession with home ownership pay off?', The Conversation.

31 Melissa Lawford, 'Has Britain's house price crash been cancelled – or is it still coming this autumn?', *Telegraph* (21 July 2020).

32 Regional price caps have been introduced as of 2021, so the maximum of £600,000 only applies in London. In other English regions, the maximum purchase price varies.

33 Merryn Somerset Webb, 'Help to Buy is building a legacy of misery', *Financial Times* (1 March 2019).

34 Leah Milner, 'Premium paid on Help to Buy homes up to 22%: Reallymoving', Mortgage Strategy (8 October 2019).

35 www.thetimes.co.uk/article/after-grenfell-why-did-fire-destroy-flats-at-worcester-park-last-year-rg5hozmsk.

36 Liam Halligan, 'The lack of home owners in the UK undermines our society', *Telegraph* (25 January 2020).

37 'Lifetime renters set to exhaust their pension pot 12 years before homeowners', TISA (11 February 2020).

38 Nick Green, 'How to save up a deposit in 6 years (or less)', Unbiased (3 September 2020).

39 'First-time buyers need 10 and a half years to save for a deposit', Hamptons International press release (22 June 2018).

40 Amy Austin, 'Pensioners have more spare cash than workers', *FT* Adviser (26 April 2019).

41 Chris Goulden, 'UK Poverty 2019/20', Joseph Rowntree Foundation (7 February 2020).

42 You can still enrol if you're under 22. Google 'Automatic enrolment if you're 21 or under' from the Money Advice Service for more information.

43 Nick Reeve, 'Auto-enrolment success masks inadequate savings rates, industry warns', *IPE* (20 June 2019).

44 'UK savers must set aside a quarter of earnings for a good retirement', Institute and Faculty of Actuaries (30 October 2019).

45 'Investing in (and for) Our Future', WEF White Paper (June 2019).

46 *Money Observer*.

47 'Show Me My Money – research paper', Interactive Investor.

48 'Workplace Pension Contributions', Scottish Widows; and Duncan Ferris, 'Aegon calls for AE contributions boost', *Pensions Age* (18 February 2020).

49 'Stepping up AE contributions could boost pension pot by £88K', Aegon (19 February 2020).

50 'Retirement Living Standards', Pensions and Lifetime Savings Association.

51 'Nest Insight launches its sidecar savings trial', Nest Insight (12 November 2018).

52 'Moments That Matter', Chartered Insurance Institute.

53 'UK pension system short-changing women, claims research by NOW: Pensions and Pensions Policy Institute', NOW: Pensions (4 March 2020).

54 Natalie Tuck, 'Global pension assets "bounce back" to hit $46.7trn – WTW', Pensions Age (10 February 2020).

55 Cristian Angeloni, 'Younger savers not aware pensions are invested', International Adviser (17 September 2020).

56 Emma Simon, 'Performance gap widens among workplace default pensions', Corporate Adviser (16 October 2019).

57 quietroom.co.uk.

58 Paul Britton and Toby Belsom, 'The Engagement Deficit', Share Action.

59 Maxime Carmignac, 'ESG could now be a "safe haven"', *FT* Adviser (11 June 2020).

60 Anthony Hilton, 'Do we actually know what ESG is? Some of the biggest index providers and rating agencies don't always agree', *Evening Standard* (3 March 2020).

61 'IMF report on sustainability', ESG Investing (11 October 2019).

62 YouGov (May 2018).

63 Hannah Gilbert and Bethan Livesey, 'Pensions for the Next Generation: Communicating What Matters', Share Action (March 2018).

64 www.annualstatement.co.uk.

65 Tanya Jefferies, 'Would you be more likely to read a pension letter if it arrived in an orange envelope? Government may borrow Swedish idea to spark savers' interest', This is Money (1 November 2019).

66 www.pensiontracingservice.com.

67 'Calastone Study Reveals Returns And Fees Are The Investment Priorities For Millennials Not Ethical Investing', Calastone.

68 Jean-Philippe Deranty, 'Work is a fundamental part of being human. Robots won't stop us doing it', The Conversation (9 December 2019).

69 'A decade of digital dependency', Ofcom (2 August 2018).

70 Catherine Price, 'Trapped – the secret ways social media is built to be addictive (and what you can do to fight back)', *Science Focus* (29 October 2018).

71 The estimated paper loss of companies listed on the Nasdaq stock exchange, the main US market for tech companies, between March 2000 and October 2002.

72 'Lessons of Survival, From the Dot-Com Attic', *The New York Times* (23 November 2008).

73 Siobhan Riding, 'Woodford crisis shines spotlight on fund supermarket "best-buy' lists", *Financial Times* (6 September 2019).

74 William Baldwin, 'Jack Bogle Is Gone, But He's Still Saving Investors $100 Billion A Year', *Forbes* (16 January 2019).

75 'Underperformance rife among active mutual fund managers', Cass Business School.

76 Alf Wilkinson, 'Active funds fail to outperform passive rivals despite Covid-19 opportunity', *Financial Times* (1 September 2020).

77 'Active or passive: Why boring may be better', Vanguard (27 December 2017).

78 Paul R. La Monica, 'The next bubble: Passive investing in ETFs', CNN (18 August 2020).

79 Jonathan Jones, 'Has your robo-adviser made you money in 2020?', *Telegraph* (24 June 2020).

80 This is based on a combination of my own research and analysis of the LangCat ISA Guide 2020.

81 This is based on the 0.22% annual fee for one of Vanguard's popular LifeStrategy funds.

82 Damien Fahy, 'Wealthsimple review – Is it the best choice for investors in the UK?', moneytothemasses.com (25 June 2020).

83 Jonathan Jones, 'Has your robo-adviser made you money in 2020?', *Telegraph* (24 June 2020).

84 'Automated investment services – our expectations', FCA (21 May 2018).

85 This bond is not covered by the FCA or the FSCS. To protect your money, Dozens places all the money you invest plus the full 12-months' interest in a separate trustee-controlled account on your behalf to pay you in the event of default.

86 Jonathan Jones, 'Has your robo-adviser made you money in 2020?', *Telegraph* (24 June 2020).

87 Anthony Morrow, 'MiFID II is making the costs of your investments clearer', *What Investment* (11 July 2019).

88 Matt Krantz, 'What $10,000 Invested In FAANG Stocks Is Worth Now', *Investor's Business Daily* (10 February 2020).

89 Simon Lambert, 'Buying shares is back in fashion but will the new wave of traders turn into investors once lockdown and the tech boom fade', This is Money (17 September 2020).

90 Richard Henderson, 'Frustrated sports punters turn to US stock market', *Financial Times* (20 May 2020).

91 Simon Lambert, 'Buying shares is back in fashion but will the new wave of traders turn into investors once lockdown and the tech boom fade', This is Money (17 September 2020).

92 Robin Wigglesworth, Richard Henderson and Eric Platt, 'The lockdown death of a 20-year-old day trader', *Financial Times* (2 July 2020).

93 Robin Wigglesworth, Richard Henderson and Eric Platt, 'The lockdown death of a 20-year-old day trader', *Financial Times* (2 July 2020).

94 *Money 101*, Episode 7, BBC.

95 Moira O'Neill, 'Investing vs gambling: a fine line to tread', *Financial Times* (16 September 2020).

96 Harry Brennan, 'How I quit my job and ended up earning £100,000 a year investing', *Telegraph* (4 March 2019).

97 Rob Langston, 'Three-quarters of UK active managers outperformed in 2019', Trustnet (18 March 2020).

98 Jemima Kelly, 'When "commission-free trading" isn't (really) free', *Financial Times* (20 February 2020).

99 Sergio Held, 'Venezuela's currency: Worth more as craft paper than as money', *Al Jazeera* (24 December 2019).

100 'The 2020 Geography of Cryptocurrency Report', Chainalysis (September 2020).

101 Alexander Lebedev, 'Cryptocurrency has the power to revolutionise a corrupt banking system', *Independent* (12 October 2020).

102 Bojan Stojkovski, 'Albanian gangs take up cryptocurrencies: "We need a new approach" say police', ZD Net (18 September 2019).

103 S. Foley, J. R. Karlsen and T. J. Putnins, 'Sex, Drugs, and Bitcoin: How Much Illegal Activity is Financed Through Cryptocurrencies', *Review of Financial Studies* 32, 1798–1853 (2019).

104 Jamie Bartlett, 'The Missing Cryptoqueen', BBC Sounds. I highly recommend this podcast.

105 Julia Kollewe, 'Bitcoin price plunges after cryptocurrency exchange is hacked', *Guardian* (11 June 2018).

106 Monty Munford, 'How I lost £25,000 when my cryptocurrency was stolen', BBC (15 August 2019).

107 James Delingpole, 'Why oh why didn't I buy more Bitcoin?', *The Spectator* (18 November 2017).

108 'How to buy Bitcoin for the First Time', eToro.

109 Interactive Investor, 'Bitcoin is the top performing asset in recent history – so should investors take it more seriously?', (18 November 2019).

110 Elle Hunt, 'What Beanie Babies taught a generation about the horrors of boom and bust', *Guardian* (19 June 2019).

111 'FCA bans the sale of crypto-derivatives to retail consumers', CFA press release (6 October 2020).

112 J. Kasper, 'Evolution of Bitcoin: Volatility comparisons with least developed countries' currencies', Working Paper (2017).

113 James Temple, 'Bitcoin mining may be pumping out as much CO_2 per year as Kansas City', *MIT Technology Review* (12 June 2019).

114 Sarah Knapton, 'Bitcoin using more electricity per transaction than a British household in two months', *Telegraph* (1 March 2020).

115 'Cryptoasset consumer research 2020', Financial Conduct Authority (30 June 2020).

116 'Cryptoassets Taskforce: final report', gov.uk (30 July 2018).

117 Sarah Guershon, 'Fake Martin Lewis ads', MoneySavingExpert.com (16 September 2020).

118 'Cryptoasset consumer research 2020', FCA Research Note (30 June 2020).

119 Georgios Panos and Tatja Karkkainen, 'Financial Literacy And Attitudes To Cryptocurrencies', Think Forward Initiative (20 February 2020).

120 Mr Money Mustache, 'So you're thinking about investing in bitcoin? Don't', *Guardian* (15 January 2018).

121 Rebecca Aydin, 'The WeWork fiasco of 2019, explained in 30 seconds', *Business Insider* (22 October 2019).

122 Louisa Clarence-Smith and John Simpson, 'Amateur investors "lose £1bn" in northern powerhouse buy-to-let schemes', *Times* (15 February 2020).

123 William Cole, 'Is YOUR copy of Harry Potter worth £75,000?', *Daily Mail* (13 October 2020).

124 Rupert Jones, 'I'm 19,050th in the queue to get my savings back', *Guardian* (17 October 2020).

125 Kristin Stoller, 'The New Beer Barons: How Two Scottish Kids Turned Wild Flavors, Crowdfunding And Plenty Of Attitude Into A $2 Billion Business', *Forbes* (14 January 2020).

126 Laura Whitcombe, 'Reckless conservatism: don't blow your fortune in cash', *The Spectator* (7 April 2016).

127 'MSCI Developed Markets Indexes', www.msci.com/developed-markets.

128 'MSCI Developed Markets Indexes', www.msci.com/developed-markets.

129 Imogen Tew, 'ESG inflows quadruple in 2020', *FT* Adviser (5 November 2020).

130 Jemma Jackson, 'What investors should do when a long-serving fund manager leaves', Interactive Investor (19 May 2020).

131 David Stevenson, 'Five more thematic ETFs for growth', Citywire (28 May 2020).

132 Madison Darbyshire, 'Psychological traps investors should be wary of', *Financial Times* (9 July 2020).

133 Tom Selby, 'How pound-cost averaging helped dampen the last two global financial shocks', AJ Bell Youinvest (22 April 2020).

Index